ALLEN CARR

Allen Carr was a chain-smoker for over 30 years. In 1983, after countless failed attempts to quit, he went from 100 cigarettes a day to zero without suffering withdrawal pangs, without using willpower and without putting on weight. He realized that he had discovered what the world had been waiting for – the Easy Way to Stop Smoking, and embarked on a mission to help cure the world's smokers.

As a result of the phenomenal success of his method, he gained an international reputation as the world's leading expert on stopping smoking and his network of clinics now spans the globe. His first book, *Allen Carr's Easy Way to Stop Smoking*, has sold over 12 million copies, remains a global bestseller and has been published in over forty different languages. Hundreds of thousands of smokers have successfully quit at Allen Carr's Easyway Clinics where, with a success rate of over 90%, he guarantees you'll find it easy to stop or your money back.

Allen Carr's Easyway method has been successfully applied to a host of issues including weight control, alcohol, debt and other addictions. A list of Allen Carr clinics appears at the back of this book. Should you require any assistance or if you have any questions, please do not hesitate to contact your nearest clinic.

For more information about Allen Carr's Easyway, please visit **www.allencarr.com**

Allen Carr's Easyway

The key that will set you free

CONTENTS

INTRODUCTION

By John Dicey, Worldwide Managing Director & Senior Therapist, Allen Carr's Easyway

For a third of a century Allen Carr chain-smoked 60 to 100 cigarettes a day. With the exception of acupuncture, he'd tried all the conventional methods to quit using willpower, nicotine products, hypnotherapy, substitutes and other gimmicks, all without success.

As he describes it: "It was like being between the devil and the deep blue sea. I desperately wanted to quit but whenever I tried I was utterly miserable. No matter how long I survived without a cigarette, I never felt completely free. It was as if I had lost my best friend, my crutch, my character, my very personality. In those days I believed there were such types as addictive personalities or confirmed smokers, and because my family were all heavy smokers, I believed that there was something in our genes that meant we couldn't enjoy life or cope with stress without smoking."

Eventually he gave up even trying to quit believing: "Once a smoker always a smoker." Then he discovered something which motivated him to try again.

"I went overnight from a hundred cigarettes a day to zero – without any bad temper or sense of loss, void or depression. On the contrary, I actually enjoyed the process. I knew I was already a non-smoker even before I had extinguished my final cigarette and I've never had the slightest urge to smoke since."

It didn't take Allen long to realize that he had discovered a method of quitting that would enable any smoker to quit.

- EASILY, IMMEDIATELY AND PERMANENTLY
- WITHOUT USING WILLPOWER, AIDS, SUBSTITUTES OR GIMMICKS
- WITHOUT SUFFERING DEPRESSION OR WITHDRAWAL SYMPTOMS
- WITHOUT GAINING WEIGHT

After using his smoking friends and relatives as guinea pigs, he gave up his lucrative profession as a qualified accountant and set up a clinic to help other smokers to quit.

He called his method "EASYWAY" and so successful has it been that there are now Allen Carr's Easyway clinics in more than 150 cities in 50 countries worldwide. Best-selling books based on his method have been translated into more than 38 languages, with more being added each year.

It quickly became clear to Allen that his method could be applied to any drug. The method has helped millions of people to quit smoking, alcohol, and other drugs, as well as to stop gambling, overeating, and overspending. The method works by unravelling the misconceptions that make people believe that they get some benefit from the very thing that's harming them.

This book applies the same method to the issue of sugar addiction and, unlike other methods, it does not require willpower.

Too good to be true? All you have to do is read the book in its entirety, follow all the instructions and you cannot fail.

I'm aware that the claims of the method's success might appear far-fetched or exaggerated, at times even outrageous. That was certainly my reaction when I first heard them. I was incredibly fortunate to attend Allen Carr's clinic in London in 1997, yet I did so under duress. I had agreed to go, at the request of my wife, on the understanding that when I walked out of the clinic and remained a smoker she would leave it at least 12 months before hassling me about stopping smoking again. No one was more surprised than I, or perhaps my wife, that Allen Carr's Easyway method set me free from my 80-a-day addiction.

I was so inspired that I hassled and harangued Allen Carr and Robin Hayley (then Managing Director and now Chairman of Allen Carr's Easyway) to let me get involved in their quest to cure the world of smoking. I was incredibly fortunate to have succeeded in convincing them to allow me to do so. Being trained by Allen Carr and Robin Hayley was one of the most rewarding experiences of my life. To be able to count Allen as not only my coach and mentor, but also my friend was an amazing honour and privilege. Allen Carr and Robin Hayley trained me well – I went on to personally treat more than 30,000 smokers at Allen's original London clinic, and be part of the team that has taken Allen's method from Berlin to Bogota, from New Zealand to New York, and from Sydney to Santiago.

Tasked by Allen to ensure that his legacy achieves its full potential we've taken Allen Carr's Easyway from videos to DVD, from clinics to apps, from computer games to audio books, to online programmes and beyond. We've a long way to go, with so many addictions and issues to apply the method to, and this book plays a special part in our quest.

The honour of adding a light editorial touch in this book to update and develop Allen's method has fallen to me. Editing Allen's work enables us to apply the most up-to-date, cutting-edge version of his method to a whole host of issues.

A decade ago you'd have been forgiven for thinking that sugar was the least of modern man's problems. Yet in 2016 the world is in the grip of what can only be described as an obesity and Type 2 diabetes epidemic. The fact that the food and drinks industry has used many of the same tactics as BIG TOBACCO in the 50s, 60s and 70s is ironic given that Allen's method is synonymous with smoking. Once you're free from sugar and enjoying the results of that freedom – infinitely better health, higher levels of energy, improved body shape and a happier, healthier lifestyle – you might be inclined to take a look at that industry (and some of the medical and scientific establishment) and wonder how on earth they convinced us into believing that "fat" was the enemy of good health as opposed to sugar. That focus, away from sugar towards fat, is something that has cost millions of lives and filled the bloated coffers of the food, drink and pharmaceutical industries to bursting.

Follow Allen Carr's instructions and you'll find it not only easy to be free from BAD SUGAR, but you'll actually enjoy the process of quitting. You won't just be free; you'll be happy to be free. That might sound too good to be true at the moment, but read on. You've got nothing to lose and absolutely everything to gain. Let me pass you into the safest of hands – over to Allen Carr.

Chapter 1

LIFE IS SWEET ENOUGH

IN THIS CHAPTER

•HOW GOOD COULD YOU FEEL? •A GLOBAL EPIDEMIC
•ADDICTION •ENJOYING WHAT YOU EAT •NO HALF MEASURES
•A METHOD THAT WORKS •PLANNING YOUR ESCAPE

This book will help you to understand the truth about BAD SUGAR and take you through a proven method to cut it out of your diet completely and permanently, without leaving you feeling deprived or requiring any willpower. In fact, it will be easy. No doubt you find that hard to believe but read on. I have only good news for you.

We all have good days and bad days. On your good days, do you ever wonder whether you could feel better? Could you have more energy perhaps? Could you lose some weight? Is there a niggling ailment that you've learned to live with but would really love to shake off? Do you feel dissatisfied with the person you see in the mirror?

Why wait until these symptoms become severe before doing something about them? If you're in the situation where your symptoms are already severe, don't panic. The key to your freedom is in your hands. The fact is, almost everybody in the world could feel infinitely better in many ways by making one simple change to their diet:

SHELVE THE SUGAR!

The fact that you are reading this book shows that you have made a decision to do something about the amount of sugar you consume. Perhaps you want to lose weight and boost your level of fitness; you may be worried about developing Type 2 diabetes, heart disease or one of the other severe medical conditions that have been linked to excessive sugar consumption; or perhaps you have read about the evils of sugar and want to protect yourself or your children before it's too late.

Most of us are hooked on sugar before we're even old enough to be aware that we're eating it. We grow up with no idea what it feels like to live life sugar-free. We assume that the lethargy we feel, the lows, the restlessness and the difficulty in controlling our moods and weight are just facts of life and we struggle on, continuing to stuff ourselves with sugar whenever we feel in need of a lift. The truth is very different.

SUGAR ADDICTS EAT THEMSELVES MISERABLE

You may also be aware that we need a certain amount of sugar in our diet for energy. In the next chapter I'll explain the difference between "good sugar", which we obtain naturally from the plants we eat, and "bad sugar", which is refined from sugar cane and other plants, stripped of their natural goodness. Easyway also classes processed carbohydrate (such as pasta) and starchy carbs (such as potato) as "BAD SUGAR". Most of the sugar we consume has no place in a healthy human diet. It is as unnatural as drinking petrol or injecting heroin into your veins.

When I refer to "eating sugar" throughout the book, please take this to mean eating or drinking BAD SUGAR.

Weighty facts

Obesity has become a global epidemic. According to the World Health Organization:

- 2.8 million people die each year as a result of being overweight or obese.
- In 2013, 42 million of the world's pre-school children were found to be overweight.
- Globally, 44 per cent of diabetes, 23 per cent of ischaemic heart disease and up to 41 per cent of certain cancers are attributable to obesity.
- In 2013 there were 382 million people suffering with diabetes. By 2016 the figure had increased to 400 million. There is no doubt that the world is in the grip of a diabetes epidemic with the number of people suffering from the condition predicted to increase to almost 600 million by 2035 unless mankind changes its lifestyle and the way it eats.
- It's not just Western society suffering. In countries

such as China and India, almost 10 per cent of adults have diabetes.
- In the UK alone there are more than 3 million people living with diabetes.

The simple truth is that BAD SUGAR is the main cause of obesity and diabetes.

Dateline 2016: in the UK, studies show that an alarming number of youngsters are suffering from serious, life-changing tooth decay caused by sugar. This is in spite of free dental check-ups and treatment for children provided for decades by the National Health Service. The same "dental decay" tragedy is occurring in youngsters from Kentucky to Cancun and from Birmingham to Brisbane. It's an indictment of education systems, parenting, and an unregulated, BAD SUGAR-pushing food industry.

WHITE DEATH

There is no secret about the ill effects of eating too much of the wrong kind of sugar. From an early age we're told that it rots our teeth (actually it's the bacteria that feed on it that cause the cavities), but in recent years the spotlight has fallen on a catalogue of more life-threatening conditions that have been linked to sugar consumption, most notably obesity and Type 2 diabetes.

It is hard, if not impossible, to find anybody who will stand up and say sugar is good for you. Yet from an early age we are brainwashed into regarding sugary foods as a treat. Sweets, cakes, biscuits, lollypops, ice cream, and chocolates – we are given them as rewards for being good! Only now are parents beginning to understand that, far from rewarding their children, they are passing on a potential death sentence.

For most people who grow up regarding sugar as a treat, it is only when they have become overweight or have been diagnosed with Type 2 diabetes, or most likely both, that they begin to see the truth. And even then they struggle to cut sugar out of their diet. Extraordinarily, people who range from "merely overweight" to being "clinically" or even "morbidly" obese continue to consume BAD SUGAR on a daily basis in suicidally large quantities without realizing the true nature of the harm it is causing them. Why should this be? How is it that BAD SUGAR that causes so much known harm continues to be consumed in such vast quantities that it is causing a health disaster on a global scale?

> BAD SUGAR = refined sugar, processed carbohydrates, and starchy carbohydrates.

HOOKED

Have you ever said to yourself, "I'll just have the one biscuit," and then found you've eaten two or three or even the whole packet? What makes you do that? Is it sheer, unadulterated pleasure?

If it is, why did you try to limit yourself to just the one in the first place? Because you were worried about the health risks? Or because you knew that if you had two it would probably lead to three and perhaps the whole packet, and then you'd suffer that guilty feeling, you'd despise yourself for your lack of self-control and you'd end up feeling miserable? All for the sake of a biscuit.

When something is a genuine pleasure, there is no need to restrict yourself in how often you enjoy it. We restrict ourselves when we sense that it might do us harm. In the case of sugar, you'd be absolutely right.

No doubt you might find it hard to accept that you don't get any pleasure from sugar. I'll explain more about that later. In the first instance, I'd like you to keep an open mind about that. Just consider the possibility that you don't get pleasure from it. Don't feel obliged to agree with that notion at this stage – merely consider it as a possibility.

So, if it isn't pleasure, why do you go back for more?

You might be surprised by the answer:

ADDICTION

You've probably heard that sugar is addictive but you may have dismissed it as no more than a theory or a joke, like calling someone who can't resist chocolate a chocaholic. No one likes to admit they're really an addict and it seems incredible to think that just about everybody on the planet is hooked on the same substance. But that is exactly how it is. We all like to think we're in control but if you really were in control you wouldn't eat the second, third and certainly not the fourth biscuit. In fact, you wouldn't eat the first either.

It's easy to see addiction in others. The junkie who sticks a needle in his arm is clearly addicted. At our specialist clinics that treat heroin addiction it's universally accepted by the addicts attending that they get absolutely no pleasure or benefit from it. They know they're only taking it to get rid of the withdrawal caused by the previous fix.

That's how addiction works. The first fix creates the craving and each subsequent fix partially relieves the withdrawal before creating another craving for the next.

Instead of curing himself by breaking the cycle, the addict seeks to get rid of his craving by taking the very thing that caused it in the first place.

It's like trying to extinguish a fire with petrol! I have no doubt that you understand what I am saying in relation to heroin addiction.

Actually that craving – which in so many cases can appear overwhelming – is only 1 per cent physical and 99 per cent mental. The actual physical withdrawal pangs from most drugs are actually extremely mild – almost imperceptible. The real discomfort is caused by a sense of deprivation that addicts suffer and is created by the brain; it's triggered by the slight physical withdrawal pangs but it is fed by brainwashing.

We believe that we need whatever it is we're addicted to in order to give us some form of pleasure or a crutch. In the early days of their addiction junkies think they get that from heroin, smokers think they get it from nicotine and sugar addicts think they get it from sugar.

The brainwashing that is partially responsible for addiction is incredibly powerful. In all likelihood you've never taken heroin, yet you no doubt believe that there must be some kind of tremendous, incredible, fantastical pleasure delivered by the drug.

That's partly because of the way it's portrayed in the movies and partly because we simply can't believe that addicts would get themselves into the position of having their bodies, their families, their careers, their very existence destroyed by a drug that actually provides no pleasure. Yet the heroin addicts that attend our clinic in London rarely need any convincing on that point.

SO HOW DOES THE ADDICTION WORK?

The Little Monster

Shortly after you consume BAD SUGAR for the first time, you experience sensations of withdrawal

This withdrawal creates a very mild, empty, slightly insecure, slightly uptight feeling – it's so mild it's almost imperceptible.

The instant you take another dose of the drug that mild, empty, insecure feeling temporarily disappears, leaving you feeling normal again. In other words, you take your second dose of BAD SUGAR merely to return to feeling how you did before the first dose.

Gradually the withdrawal feelings return, and we get that very mild, empty, slightly insecure, slightly uptight feeling again. A lifetime's chain has started.

In other addictions this process is so subtle that the person taking the drug isn't even aware that it's happening.

It's the same with BAD SUGAR – but with one key difference. With BAD SUGAR, we've already been through the process of getting addicted before we're even capable of conscious thought!

SUGAR BABIES

Unlike almost every other addictive drug on this planet the people who deliver us into this addiction – the original pushers – are the people who care about us and love us most: our parents and guardians.

By the time we're capable of conscious thought we've already been addicted to BAD SUGAR for years!

It's as if it created a Little Monster inside your body that feeds on BAD SUGAR. If you don't feed it, it complains, creating an unsettled feeling. Feed it, and the feeling disappears for a while, before returning a while later.

When you break free from BAD SUGAR addiction, you starve that Little Monster to death. It's a weak pathetic monster, but it acts as a trigger for a bigger monster.

The Big Monster

From birth we're not only fed BAD SUGAR by our loved ones, but also brainwashed into believing that we get some kind of benefit or crutch from it. That it is some kind of treat or reward or that it's essential for our energy levels. The Little Monster seems to confirm this. Each time you consume BAD SUGAR and that empty, insecure, slightly uptight feeling disappears for a while, you do feel less insecure, and less uptight than a moment before. It feels like a boost. Like a heroin addict who has just had their fix.

It's the belief that we get some kind of benefit from the drug that creates the awful cravings when we try to quit. In other words, that terrible feeling of deprivation is caused by a thought process rather than by actual physical withdrawal from the drug.

The physical withdrawal (the Little Monster) never really changes and it's incredibly mild. It's the thought process that it triggers along with the brainwashing (the Big Monster) that causes the unpleasant cravings.

Understanding Easyway kills the Big Monster. Starving the Little Monster of BAD SUGAR kills it quickly and ensures you never have to suffer it again.

AN ADDICTION FROM BIRTH

For most of us, addiction is a dirty word associated with potent substances and sometimes controlled by strict laws. With most addictions we can look back and identify a moment in time when the addiction took hold, usually in our late teens or early twenties. So it seems incongruous to cast BAD SUGAR – something we've consumed since we were babies – in the same light.

But it is not unheard of for an addiction to take hold before we are even aware we are consuming the substance. Some babies are born addicted to heroin or crack cocaine. It's a tragic consequence of a mother who's hooked on the drug during pregnancy.

Huge resources are pitched against the scourge of illegal drugs because the world recognizes the horrors of heroin or crack addiction. Yet BAD SUGAR is not afforded the same attention, despite the fact that obesity, heart disease and diabetes account for many million more deaths each year than heroin.

The point is, you need to forget your preconceptions about addiction and understand how it works and that it applies to BAD SUGAR.

Only when you can accept that you are addicted to sugar can you begin the process of freeing yourself. It is important to accept that you do not control your intake of BAD SUGAR, it controls you, and the only way to break that hold is to

STOP TAKING IT ALTOGETHER

ENJOY WHAT YOU EAT

A common thread in all addictions is the fear that life without what we perceive to be our little pleasure or crutch will be miserable. Talk to people about cutting sugar out of their diet and the common response will be:

"But you've got to enjoy eating."

The assumption is that a diet without BAD SUGAR will be unenjoyable. This couldn't be further from the truth. In my book *Lose Weight Now*, I make the following claim:

Eat as much of your favourite foods as you want, whenever you want, as often as you want, and be the exact weight you want to be, without dieting, special exercise, using willpower or feeling deprived.

To many, this seems too good to be true. By the time they finish the book, they realize that it is entirely true.

There are two key words in that claim: dieting and willpower. Most methods that promise to help you control your diet rely on willpower. As I will explain later in the book, any method that relies on willpower actually makes it harder, if not impossible, to succeed.

This method does not rely on willpower at all. Neither is it a diet. The diets that you may have tried in the past and that have failed you are temporary fixes that actually have an adverse effect. It has been found that most people who diet eventually end up putting on weight.

This method is not a temporary fix, it is a solution for life. It works by changing the way you think about the food you eat, removing the brainwashing that has been with you from birth and replacing it with the truth. Once you have changed your mindset towards food, changing the way you eat is easy. You don't have to deprive yourself of anything. You will enjoy every meal. And you will look amazing, feel fitter and feel infinitely more energetic into the bargain.

WHY IT HAS TO BE EASY

If someone tried to fool you into believing that you could have just a little bit of heroin every now and then, would you be tempted to try it? Of course you wouldn't, because you know that there is no such thing as just a little heroin every now and then. One dose leads to another and another and another. The tendency is always to take more.

And anyway, you know that there is no incredible pleasure in taking heroin. Don't believe the "Tarantino-esque", glamourized, Hollywood hype awarded to heroin that gives the impression that it provides some form of incredible pleasure. As mentioned already, the vast majority of heroin addicts who attend our clinics openly acknowledge that they take the drug merely in an attempt to feel "normal" rather than for any pleasure or high or genuine benefit. The same goes for cocaine addicts and in fact addicts of every other Class A drug that seek our help.

The same applies to sugar.

Perhaps you picked up this book hoping it would help you to reduce your BAD SUGAR intake to a healthy level. Let's be quite clear about this: with BAD SUGAR there is no healthy level other than zero. Anything more than that is not only unhealthy, it will keep you hooked so you will end up increasing the amount you consume. The aim of this book is to help you get free of BAD SUGAR altogether.

Perhaps you still think that will require immense reserves of willpower. In fact, it takes more willpower to attempt to cut down than it does to cut it out completely. Only by reducing your intake to zero will you free yourself from the addiction. It's remaining addicted that makes it hard.

The same is true of smoking and other drugs. Would you consider someone who cuts down from 30 a day to 10 a day to have freed themselves from cigarettes? It takes immense willpower to cut down because the tendency with all addictive drugs is always to take more. You're constantly fighting the urge to have another fix. Eventually, the addict cracks and ends up taking even more of the drug than they were in the first place. Cutting down makes a drug seem more precious, not less. That is how addiction works. People think it is hard to quit smoking, but it's really very easy... if you know how. It's the people who use the willpower method who find it hard.

> The "Willpower method" refers to any other method of treating drug addiction that leaves the addict believing that they are sacrificing some sort of pleasure or crutch and they therefore have to apply willpower, every day, for the rest of their lives, to fight the urge to take the drug.

The only way to free yourself from the tyranny of BAD SUGAR is to recognize that it does absolutely nothing for you whatsoever and cut it out of your diet completely. This book will enable you to do so easily, painlessly and permanently. Not only that, it will allow you to actually enjoy the process.

Let this be the first day of an exciting adventure: the day you start preparing yourself to be free. All you need to do is follow the instructions. In fact, your first instruction is:

FOLLOW ALL THE INSTRUCTIONS

You can spend a lifetime trying to break into a safe and still not succeed. But if you know the correct combination or have a key, it's ridiculously easy. Lose the key or miss one part of the combination and you'll fail.

This book contains the key, the combination of information you need in order to be free. It will allow you to escape.

This method is called Easyway. To find it easy we must achieve a frame of mind whereby whenever you think about BAD SUGAR or a BAD SUGAR product you have a sense of freedom and relief that you don't consume it anymore. That's the only way to become, and remain, truly free. Changing, or more accurately correcting, your perception of BAD SUGAR will actually be an exciting, eye-opening and positive experience. No doubt you find that hard to believe, but, read on, you have absolutely nothing to lose and everything to gain.

No doubt you might have experienced countless attempts to cut down, control or eliminate BAD SUGAR from your diet and experienced varying degrees of deprivation, misery and failure. This time, it is going to be different. Don't expect it to be hard. I'll explain why it isn't going to be hard in due course.

Let's cast aside all feelings of doom and gloom. There is no need to be miserable. You are about to achieve something marvellous. See your journey through this book as it really is, an exciting, positive process. Just think how proud you'll feel when you're free.

I can't overstate the importance of keeping an open mind. Some people believe my method is a form of brainwashing. Nothing could be further from the truth. It's actually counter-brainwashing, correcting and reversing beliefs that, from birth, you have regarded as fact. Question what you think you know about BAD SUGAR. Question what society and convention have led you to believe to be true. Question what you think you know about addiction in general. If you do that, you cannot fail.

A METHOD THAT WORKS

Whatever your reason for picking up this book, you have already established one important fact in your mind: BAD SUGAR is your enemy. In Chapter 2, I will talk in more detail about the different types of sugar, about the "good" sugar your body needs for fuel and the "bad" sugar that causes nothing but harm. For now, let's just focus on the aim of this book: to conquer your addiction to sugar.

This method was first conceived as a cure for smoking, a way to help people overcome nicotine addiction. I was a heavy smoker, a 60–100 a day addict who had tried and failed to quit on countless occasions. I came to believe I was genetically predisposed to being a smoker and, therefore, the only way I could quit would be through the application of tremendous willpower. It's that misconception that prevents smokers who don't use Easyway from quitting.

My endless failed attempts to quit had convinced me that I

lacked the necessary willpower and was, therefore, condemned to suffer the misery of being a smoker for the rest of my life. But one day, a chance remark opened my eyes to the truth. I had gone to see a hypnotherapist in one last, desperate attempt to find a cure and, while the treatment did not provide the cure, a word the hypnotherapist used gave me the key. That word was "addiction". It was like a light bulb going on in my brain: I didn't smoke because I wanted to; I smoked because I was hooked.

I knew there and then that I was cured. I came home and proclaimed to my wife, Joyce, that I was going to cure the world of smoking, and so I set about creating Easyway. I never felt the desire to smoke another cigarette.

Easyway has helped tens of millions of people around the world to quit smoking and to gain freedom from other problems and addictions, including alcohol, gambling, debt, fear of flying and overeating. The method has gained a devoted following almost entirely on the strength of word of mouth, for one simple reason:

IT WORKS

It works not by forcing you through a painful withdrawal process or demanding huge resources of willpower. It works simply by helping you to see the truth.

Perhaps you think you already know all there is to know about the harmful effects of sugar, and yet you still consume it. Smokers also know all about the harmful effects of smoking, yet they still go to incredible lengths to feed their addiction. When

I talk about the truth, I don't mean the truth that sugar is bad for you – everybody knows that; I mean the truth that **REFINED SUGAR, PROCESSED AND STARCHY CARBOHYDRATES, DO ABSOLUTELY NOTHING FOR YOU WHATSOEVER**.

YOUR WAY OUT

You may be thinking, "If this method makes it so easy to cut out sugar, why don't you just give me the key and let me get on with it?" Please be patient. You will find your escape very soon and the short time it takes to read this book will seem like a very good investment for the lifetime of freedom you will gain.

As mentioned already, the method works like the combination lock on a safe. I can give you the instructions but unless you follow all of them in the right order, the combination won't work and the lock will remain firmly closed.

REMEMBER MY FIRST INSTRUCTION: FOLLOW ALL THE INSTRUCTIONS

You may be tempted to skip to the end of the book to see how the method works. If you do that, the method will not work. It is essential that you read the entire book from start to finish and don't miss anything out.

Throughout your life, you have been the victim of brainwashing that has given you a false idea about sugar and what it does for you. We need to unravel that brainwashing and replace it with the truth.

Remember, you picked up this book because you want to do

something about the sugar you consume. Any method you may have tried in the past has not worked so you are hoping this method will be different. Rest assured, it is. And it works. All you have to do is follow all the instructions.

DON'T CHANGE ANYTHING YET

While you're reading this book, there is no need to change the way you eat. The time will come when you no longer feel any need or desire for sugar, but until that time comes it's important that you carry on consuming it as normal. So please keep consuming sugar in the way you usually do, without changing your diet in any way, until I instruct you otherwise.

SUMMARY

- Because we're hooked on sugar from an early age, we regard it as normal. It's anything but.

- Addiction and brainwashing are what makes us continue to consume sugar, despite knowing all the harm it causes us.

- With addiction we try to relieve our craving by taking the very thing that caused it.

- Cutting down is pointless. It's also incredibly hard.

- Quitting the easy way means quitting completely – the great news is that it is EASY.

- It does not require willpower.

- Follow all the instructions.

Chapter 2

NATURE'S GUIDE

Our love of sweet things should not be seen as a weakness. It is what helped us to survive for millions of years. Only when man tried to outsmart Nature by creating a substance that deceived his fellow humans did the love of sweetness become our undoing.

Have you ever observed a squirrel going about its business? This common creature is a wonder of nature. It can scale a vertical wall in seconds, leap from branch to branch, run along a fence, even walk a tightrope! Have you ever seen a squirrel that has lost the physical ability to do these things? You don't see overweight squirrels, do you?

If you have ever watched a squirrel eat nuts you will understand why. Put a bowl of nuts in front of most humans and they will keep eating until the bowl is empty. Not so a squirrel. It will eat what it needs and hide the rest for later. This is brilliant forward planning, vital for an animal that can never be sure where its next meal is coming from, but how does it know to do it? Its brain is tiny, yet when it comes to this aspect of survival it appears to outsmart most humans.

Does the squirrel apply willpower? Does it know that if it eats all the nuts it will get too fat to scale the wall and it may starve in the future, and so deny itself the pleasure of gorging itself? Surely not. Yet when you look at the animal kingdom, there is evidence everywhere of the same resistance to overeating. Every wild creature on Earth, apart from humans, maintains a physique suited to the lifestyle and environment in which it lives. Even apparently fat animals like hippos and walruses are designed to be that shape because it suits their lifestyle and environment. They are, to all intents and purposes, uniform in their physique.

Think of the amazing images we see on television of animals in large groups. It could be a school of fish, a herd of buffalo, a flock of geese. Their individual sizes may differ slightly, but they are all the same shape, the same proportion. Other than the very old, the very young and lame there are none that lag behind the others. And certainly none that are weighed down by an oversized belly caused by overeating. There are only three types of animal on the planet that have weight problems: humans, the domesticated animals whose eating habits humans control and the wild animals whose diet has been contaminated by the addictive food waste discarded by humans. There is no greater example of the latter than suburban pigeons in the UK. The incidence of obesity in the human population over the past 30 years seems to be mirrored in the pigeon population.

So every other species on Earth eats as much of their favourite foods as they want, as often as they want to, without being overweight! How do they do it? Does the squirrel, the fish, the buffalo spend its life applying willpower to stop itself overeating? Of course it doesn't. All of these animals know instinctively what they should and shouldn't eat.

AND SO DID WE ONCE UPON A TIME!

Our ancestors didn't need nutritionists to tell them how to keep in shape. But our intellect has led us to think differently, to the point where we no longer know what to think when it comes to eating. There have been so many new diets, each one apparently contradicting the principles of the one before. No wonder we're confused. We get bombarded with technical information and stats that even scientists, it seems, don't fully understand. If they did, surely one of them would have devised a diet that works by now.

THE ONLY INFORMATION WE REALLY NEED IS THE INFORMATION WE WERE BORN WITH: INSTINCT

Instinct, not intellect, is what tells us what and when to eat, as I will explain later in the book. For every creature on the planet the menu is different, tailored specifically for them. It is an ingenious plan that we refer to as Nature's Guide and it is the best diet plan you will ever get.

Remember the claim from *Lose Weight Now*: Eat as much of your favourite food as you want, as often as you want to and be the exact weight you want to be, without dieting, special exercise, using willpower or feeling deprived. You may have thought it sounded too good to be true. When is life ever that simple? Think about 99.9 per cent of the animal kingdom who all find it that simple. It has to be worth a closer look to try to understand how they do it.

You might point to the difficulty animals have in finding food, the lengths they have to go to to catch it or harvest it and bring it back to their families. Yes, food is often scarce and that can restrict their consumption and even lead to starvation. But what about when food is abundant? Why don't you see animals gorging themselves and becoming obese?

THE WRONG KIND OF SUGAR

As a species, we are predisposed to liking sweet things for a good reason. Our bodies and minds need sugar for fuel. Carbohydrate, in the form of glucose, is the energy source that feeds our brains, muscles and other vital functions, and we get the glucose we need from the sugars found naturally in plants. Nature's Guide makes sure we are drawn to the best sources of natural sugar by making them sweet and giving us a taste for that sweetness.

Perhaps you're thinking it would have been better if humans had been designed to like bitter foods; then we wouldn't be so attracted to sugary foods. But man's taste for sweetness evolved millions of years before he ever tasted a cake, sweet or fizzy drink. The food industry has used refined sugar in an attempt to replicate the taste of our favourite foods. If we had been designed with a taste for bitter food, the food industry would have come up with a different product that tasted bitter.

Refined sugar has been around for more than two thousand years, but until relatively recently it was a rarity available only to the very rich. In the 18th century the production of sugar from sugar cane exploded on the back of slavery and the Industrial Revolution. This is when it became widely available to the masses.

Rationing during the Second World War created a powerful mystique for sugar, making it something of a rarity. Ever since, the consumption of refined sugar has ballooned out of all proportion. Today the sugar market in the West has little room left for growth – we are literally saturated with sugar – but the rest of the world is rapidly catching up. No wonder there is a global diabetes epidemic!

- At the beginning of the 20th century, the world's population consumed an average of 11.2lb/5.1kg of sugar per capita per year.
- Today we consume 46.3lb/21kg per capita – more than four times as much!
- The American Heart Association recommends no more than 9.5 teaspoons of sugar per day; while, according to *Forbes* magazine, the average adult consumes 22 teaspoons per day and the average child 32 teaspoons of sugar every single day.

The biggest culprit is crystallized sugar from sugar cane and sugar beet, but other products such as high fructose corn syrup, used predominantly in food manufacturing, have added to the problem. While all BAD SUGAR comes from natural sources, it is far from natural by the time we come to consume it. The refining process is very similar to the way the coca plant is refined into cocaine, or poppy seeds refined into heroin. Starting with a sugar cane plant, the refining strips away its fibre, vitamins and minerals, leaving behind a white, crystalline substance that is very sweet and soluble and can, therefore, be easily added to other foods to deceive us into thinking that we are eating foods that are good. Remember, our instincts drive us towards sweet, fresh, nutritious fruit and vegetables.

Refined sugar is referred to as an "empty carb", which means it contains barely any nutritional value but is high in carbohydrate. Eating too much of it means the body is taking in an excess of carbohydrate – far more than it can burn – and this excess is turned into fat. Because it contains no nutritional value, refined sugar products do not satisfy hunger, and so create a need to eat more. The tendency is to eat more and more sugar.

Send a bowl of oranges around an office and people will help themselves to one and enjoy it, leaving any left over in the bowl. Have you ever seen that happen with a tray of cakes, biscuits or chocolates?

So why the tendency to eat more and more? This is because refined sugar also has a disastrous effect on your blood sugar level, creating false highs and causing it to crash. And this is the pattern that leads to addiction.

You can quickly understand how refined sugar has become the most harmful substance in the developed world. Heroin and cocaine addicts are relatively rare; BAD SUGAR addiction is a blight that afflicts almost everyone at some point in their life.

DIABETES

Diabetes is a condition caused by the malfunction of insulin, the hormone that regulates the flow of glucose in the bloodstream. Type 1 diabetes occurs when the body does not produce the insulin it needs. This type tends to develop at a young age. Type 2 diabetes usually develops later in life, although cases among children have seen a global increase, accounting for almost half of all newly diagnosed cases in some countries. It occurs when the body stops using insulin effectively, i.e. the cells develop a resistance to insulin.

The effects of Type 2 diabetes, which is in almost every case not only preventable, but reversible, are catastrophic.

In the case of smoking, decades of publicity educating us about the catastrophic health effects of that addiction mean we're much better informed than the smokers in the 1930s, 1940s or 1950s. The tobacco companies did their absolute best, by legal and illegal means, to conceal the truth and deceive generations of smokers. Are the same kind of powerful commercial forces with vested interests behind our lack of knowledge regarding the effects of bombarding our bodies with hourly doses of BAD SUGAR?

Even mildly raised glucose levels that do not cause any symptoms can lead to long-term damage. Obesity and diabetes greatly increase the danger of stroke and heart disease. Blood vessels become clogged up and narrowed by fatty substances resulting in poor blood supply to your heart – potentially causing angina and increasing the chances that a blood vessel in your heart or brain will become blocked – leading to heart attack or stroke.

Diabetes can cause nerve damage, amputation of affected areas such as feet, blindness and organ failure, e.g. kidney failure

Can you imagine carrying on eating and drinking as you are now, knowing that you are headed towards that kind of fate? No wonder the food conglomerates want to keep it quiet.

The Easyway method prides itself on not using scare tactics and I thought long and hard about whether to include the above information in this book. Yet I was compelled to do so because so few of us are aware of the toll (in most cases entirely avoidable) that obesity and Type 2 diabetes takes. We only become truly aware of it when the doctor gives us the bad news.

Whether you suffer from it or are concerned that you are headed towards it, I don't want you to use this information to be frightened. I want you to understand it then put it behind you and enjoy the release from any concern when you escape to freedom.

The World Health Organization has reported a global diabetes epidemic, with around 400 million sufferers worldwide and deaths from the condition expected to increase by 50 per cent in the next 10 years. But this is not a death sentence that the world cannot avoid,

> **TYPE 2 DIABETES IS PREVENTABLE AND CURABLE!**
> The rapid increase in diabetes, 90 per cent of which is Type 2 diabetes, is attributed to the rise in obesity and lack of exercise, which in turn is almost exclusively attributable to the increase in the amount of BAD SUGAR we consume.

Think of the resources and education programmes deployed in the face of the AIDS epidemic in the 1980s. Isn't it surprising that the same kind of approach isn't being deployed against the obesity and Type 2 diabetes epidemic fuelled by BAD SUGAR? Powerful forces are at work here, every bit as underhanded, Machiavellian and downright evil as BIG TOBACCO in the late 20th century!

A NEW OUTLOOK

Lose Weight Now explains how overeating is a consequence of incorrect eating. By eating the wrong type of foods we deprive ourselves of the nutrients our bodies need and so never properly satisfy our hunger. This leads us to eat more and so the fat piles on. What *Lose Weight Now* didn't tackle sufficiently was sugar addiction. That wasn't ever the intention of the book. It's an incredibly effective way of gaining control of your weight, but it simply wasn't written to tackle sugar addiction. The book you hold in your hand now has all the answers you need. Follow all of the instructions and you'll not only be freed from your sugar addiction, but take complete control of your weight and physique too.

BAD SUGAR is the chief culprit among the "bad foods" that make up the average human diet. Perhaps you don't think you're a sugar addict. Next time you are shopping check the labels on every item of food and drink before you put them in your shopping trolley. Have a shopping basket to hand also. If the product contains BAD SUGAR, put it in the basket. If it contains no sugar, put it in the trolley. Remember that's not just sugar per se, but processed carbohydrate, wheat products and starchy carbs such as potato, pasta, rice, and bread.

Even if you already accept that you are addicted to sugar, this would be a useful exercise. You may be surprised by the number of foods that contain BAD SUGAR. Even savoury dishes that you do not associate with sweetness, such as pizzas, packets of crisps and pretty much any ready-made meal and jar of sauce contain significant levels of BAD SUGAR. That's why they're so popular. It's the BAD SUGAR that fools us into thinking they are tasty and our addiction to BAD SUGAR that has us act against our true instincts.

IF THE ITEMS CONTAINING BAD SUGAR WERE REMOVED FROM THE SHELVES OF SUPERMARKETS ONLY 20 PER CENT OF THE STOCK WOULD REMAIN ON SALE!

In order to make sure you are no longer fooled by the effects of refined sugar, we need to make sure you see it for what it is:

A BLAND SUBSTANCE THAT THROWS YOUR METABOLISM INTO CHAOS AND DOES ABSOLUTELY NOTHING FOR YOU WHATSOEVER

To achieve this, it is essential that you follow all the instructions.

SECOND INSTRUCTION: KEEP AN OPEN MIND

It's rare to meet a person who doesn't claim to be open-minded. You need to go a step further than that. You need to be prepared to challenge everything that you currently believe to be true, to accept that you may have been misled and that even the most authoritative sources of information could turn out to be false. After all, think of all the dietary "facts" that get disproven a few years later. The only way to really see the truth is to open your mind and allow your instincts to take over.

SAY WHAT YOU SEE

Take a look at the two tables opposite, one square, one rectangular.

If you were told that the dimensions of each table are exactly the same, you'd be sceptical, wouldn't you?

You've already accepted that it's one square table and one rectangular one because that's what you were told and it tallies with what you see. However, the fact is they are both identical. Take a ruler and measure them. Extraordinary, isn't it!

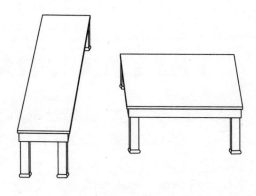

The point of showing you this illusion is to demonstrate how our minds can be easily tricked into accepting as true something that is false. When you eat a cake or a chocolate bar, you believe you are getting some form of pleasure from it, but what if that turned out to be false?

In order to open your mind, it is first necessary to accept that it has been closed.

SUMMARY

- Nature's Guide tells us what to eat and when.
- The only species that have weight problems are humans, their domesticated animals, and wild animals whose diets have been contaminated by humans' addictive junk food.
- Our intellect overrides the wisdom of our instincts.
- Refined sugar was invented in an attempt to replicate our favourite foods.
- BAD SUGAR is any product containing refined sugar or processed carbohydrate or starchy carbohydrate.
- Keep an open mind – question everything.

Chapter 3

THE BRAINWASHING

IN THIS CHAPTER
•THE SHAME OF OVEREATING •WHO CHOOSES WHAT YOU EAT?
•FAVOURITE FOODS •WHY WE CONTINUE TO OVEREAT
•DIETS DON'T WORK •THE THIRD INSTRUCTION

It is a myth that the food we eat is a matter of free choice. We are controlled in our eating from before we are even born.

A comment often made about people with a weight problem is that they "love their food". That would appear to be the case, and most people to whom this applies would claim that they enjoy food, yet they spend a lot of time feeling miserable because of food. People who are overweight know they overeat and that is not a good feeling. At best it can make you feel guilty; at worst it turns into self-loathing.

Overeaters, the term applies to a huge number of people in the world, feel ashamed of their inability to control the amount they eat. The person who is tempted by one biscuit and ends up devouring the whole packet; the person who finishes the leftover cake on the children's plates after the birthday party; the person who takes a box of chocolates to bed and scoffs the lot – they all end up feeling the same way: bloated, dissatisfied and ashamed.

But overeaters should not feel ashamed, because the "choices" they make when it comes to eating are not free choices at all. They are the result of a lifetime's brainwashing.

MOST OF THE MEALS YOU'VE CONSUMED SINCE THE DAY YOU WERE BORN WEREN'T CHOSEN BY YOU

So, if you haven't been the one in control, why should you feel guilty or ashamed about the way your eating habits have evolved?

If you followed the advice in the last chapter to read the labels of all the food you buy, you will be aware how much added sugar, processed and starchy carbohydrate there is in this diet you have been conditioned to eat. You may find that daunting. If you are to cut out all added sugar and processed and starchy carbs from your diet, what will you be left with?

Rest assured, once you have changed your mindset and rediscovered the pleasure of eating according to Nature's Guide, you will find you have more choice and variety in the food you eat than you have now. As things stand, you know there is something wrong with your eating habits but you don't know how to change them. But you are going to take charge of what you eat.

The first thing to get clear is that nobody is imposing this change on you. You are taking control and changing a situation that you're not happy with for the simple and purely selfish reason that you will enjoy life more.

There is no need for the doom and gloom that people usually feel whenever they try to solve their weight problem because you are not going on a diet: you are not going to deprive yourself of anything or force yourself through a gruelling physical challenge. Allen Carr's Easyway is different. It requires no willpower, nor does it restrict you to food you don't enjoy, nor require you to follow a programme of exercise. All you have to do is understand and follow the method and you will find yourself automatically changing your eating habits and enjoying the process.

For the first time in your life, you will genuinely be choosing what you eat.

WHAT'S YOUR FAVOURITE?

The claim that you can eat as much of your favourite food as you want, whenever you want, is often greeted with scepticism. When you then learn that you are required to change your attitude to food, you may think I'm simply changing the definition of the word "favourite". I'm not. However, it is true that, if you follow the method as instructed, you will see that the foods you regard as your favourites now may no longer be your favourites by the end.

But you will not feel conned; you will feel enlightened. Your favourite foods will be the ones that taste best and do most for you.

Think back to the optical illusion in the previous chapter. What you thought were two different-sized tables turned out to be identical. You opened your mind and allowed yourself to see the truth. Let's re-examine your favourite foods in the same way.

Judging by the fact that you're reading this book, we can assume that the foods you consider to be your favourites are not making you happy. What kind of favourite is it that makes you unhappy? You might argue that the unhappiness comes afterwards, while it's the wonderful taste of these foods that makes them your favourites. Taste, however, is changeable and it can easily be confused.

Many foods that society regards as luxuries taste revolting to begin with. Oysters, for example. Who honestly enjoys an oyster at the first time of asking? The same applies to caviar, foie gras, blue cheese and a whole host of other so-called delicacies that often taste repugnant to anyone trying them for the first time.

The beautiful truth is that the foods that taste best straight away are also the best for you. If you find this hard to believe, it's because you've been conditioned by the food industry into thinking the best tasting foods are the ones that you know to be bad for you.

Have you ever eaten a cake and really focused on the flavours in your mouth? If you were told that the butter in the icing was made from rat milk, how do you think that would change your perception of the taste? I bet you'd spit it out pretty fast. But why? What logic dictates that a cow, which spends its life covered in mud, excrement and flies, produces tastier, cleaner milk than a rat?

Don't worry, you're not going to be told to eat rat for the rest of your life. The point is that the way you *think* something tastes is influenced by brainwashing, much more than what you perceive with your own senses. And this brainwashing begins from the day you're born.

TAKE WHAT YOU'RE GIVEN AND LIKE IT

From day one, your eating habits have been controlled by others. Who decided whether you were breast-fed or fed from the bottle?

Who decided it was time to wean you on to solids, and what solids to give you? Who bought the groceries when you were growing up? Who chose what you could have for breakfast? Who drew up the school lunch menu? Who planned and cooked the evening meal?

Even as an adult your options would have been controlled by others. How much choice is there in the staff canteen? And even if you're the one who cooks the dinner, you are still influenced by your budget, a lifetime's brainwashing via advertising, what's available and the tastes you've "acquired" as a result of all the conditioning as you were growing up.

Your eating habits are the result of parental influence and restricted choice, both offered by people who have themselves been conditioned in the same way. The result is a culture of brainwashing that has become so established that, like the table illusion, we can't see through it unless it is pointed out to us.

The beauty is, though, that once you do see through it, you can never go back to being fooled by it again.

You might think the main meals of the day aren't your problem – it's the snacks you eat in between. The sweets, the potato crisps and chocolate bars you pick up on impulse at the till when you're waiting to pay for something else: is that not an exercise in free will?

Absolutely not. Your desire for those sweets, crisps or that chocolate bar is triggered by an association that's been fixed in your mind by brainwashing. The junk food advertisers want to sell as much of their products as possible and there's no limit to the innuendos they will use to make you want to buy. Their job is to create the impression that this sugar product gives you energy, or kudos or in some cases even heightens sex appeal! Some of their junk is even sold at certain times of year, as if it's a seasonal product like fruit! Once the false belief is planted in your mind, any association can spark your desire.

THIS ISN'T CHOICE, IT'S BRAINWASHING

Brainwashing also controls the amount we eat. In most cultures we are expected to eat any food that somebody else has prepared for us, and to leave nothing behind, otherwise it is deemed impolite. But who actually decides how much they put on the plate in the first place? If you're the one doing the serving, don't you tend to put more on the plate than you might consider sufficient because you don't wish to appear mean?

The feast is a custom observed all over the world, a celebration marked with food, and lots of it. Christmas Day is an orgy of eating from start to finish, our poor stomachs bombarded with a cocktail of crisps, snacks, fish, meat, rich puddings, cream, alcohol in various forms, cake, chocolate, biscuits and all sorts of other confectionery. Any fresh fruit or vegetables we might add to the mix has to sit on this mass of stodge as it festers in our digestive juices. We inevitably end the day feeling lethargic, bloated and uncomfortable, our organs struggling to cope with the overload and the toxic surplus turning to fat.

And yet the next year we're back doing it again. Why?

WHY WE CONTINUE TO OVEREAT

You would think that an experience like the Christmas blow-out would be enough to stop us ever overeating again, yet we repeat the experience year after year. And it doesn't stop at Christmas. For many people, Christmas is just an obvious example of an all year round problem. It's clear that the discomfort of the experience is not enough to put us off. There is something else compelling us to eat more.

With addictions like smoking and drinking there is an initial period where we find the taste and smell repulsive and our instincts tell us to stop. But we don't stop, we persevere until we are no longer sensitive to the taste and smell. We put ourselves through this because we want to be like our role models. If they went through it, so must we and we are convinced we will get our reward. We call it "acquiring the taste". In truth, we are acquiring a loss of taste. We are subjecting our senses to a poison against which they build up an immunity, just as rats build an immunity to rat poison. In time the cigarette or the alcoholic drink no longer tastes foul, but it's not the cigarette or the drink that has changed, it's us. We have overridden Nature's warning signs and wandered into a trap.

NATURE'S WARNING LIGHT

The way we deal with pain is a good example of how our intellect overrides our instinct. Say, after eating all that junk at Christmas, you develop a toothache. The first thing you do is take a painkiller. The pain subsides and you feel better, but does that mean the tooth is now

OK? Not at all. The pain has just been suppressed and will inevitably return with a vengeance.

You feel pain for a reason: it tells your brain and body that there's a problem that needs sorting out. By suppressing the pain and dealing with the symptom rather than the cause, you prevent your body from responding to the problem appropriately.

If the oil warning light comes on in your car, what do you do? Remove the bulb from the warning indicator? Or pull over and top up the oil? Both actions will stop the oil light from flashing; only one will prevent the engine from seizing up.

Unlike other addictions, we get hooked on sugar before we are aware we are even eating it. There is no period of adjustment. By the time we reach adulthood we are already convinced that we derive some sort of pleasure or crutch from foods containing refined sugar and processed and starchy carbohydrate. And yet whenever we eat them we never feel entirely satisfied. We eat until we are bloated.

WE CONTINUE TO OVEREAT BECAUSE WE ARE CHASING AN IMPOSSIBLE GOAL

Let's call that goal "satisfaction". Satisfaction is the feeling we get when we feed our hunger with nutritious, delicious food. It is the feeling of the body's demands being met. When we eat refined sugar or processed or starchy carbohydrates we never meet our body's demands. The nutrients we require are simply not delivered – they're absent from the "food" we're eating. Instead we get a sugar rush followed quickly by a low. This low is an uncomfortable feeling that we interpret as a desire for food – a false hunger. And instead of feeding it with nutritious foods that will satisfy any genuine hunger we may have, we try to feed it with what we think are our favourite foods: more junk.

And so the cycle goes on. Eating junk creates a low, which we try to relieve with more junk, which causes another low, etc etc.

THE ONLY WAY TO STOP THE CYCLE
IS TO STOP EATING JUNK

Think about the reasons why you overeat. They are very similar to those given by a smoker for smoking or a drinker for drinking:
- Boredom – "It's something to do and it keeps my mind occupied."
- Sadness – "It helps me forget that I'm alone."
- Stress – "It helps me to switch off and forget about my worries."
- Routine – "It's just what I do at certain times of day."
- Reward – "It's my little treat."

Happiness doesn't come into it. Sure, we mark happy occasions with cakes or chocolates, but that is nothing more than a custom.

Our happiness on these occasions doesn't create a need or desire for that cake or chocolate. In fact, it is when we are happiest that our desire for eating junk is lowest. Think of all the cake that gets left behind at a wedding.

Addicts often talk about their "drug" in terms of "reward", but that too is the result of brainwashing. Why would you reward yourself with something that could kill you? We are brought up being told sweets are a treat: we are given them when we are really good. So naturally we grow up regarding sweets as a reward. If we were given an apple when we were good, and only when we were good, we would grow up seeing apples as a treat.

SOMETHING WONDERFUL IS ABOUT TO HAPPEN

Addicts aren't stupid; they know all the pitfalls. And they know deep down that their "drug" is not a reward; it is destroying their life. They only kid themselves otherwise because they are caught in an ingenious trap. That trap is called addiction and I will look in more detail at how it works in the next chapter. First, I need to make sure you are in the right frame of mind.

Remember what you are trying to achieve: to free yourself from your addiction to sugar, help yourself to enjoy every meal and make you feel better than you've ever felt before. Your happiness is the primary aim of this book.

All your bloated Christmases are behind you. And let's be honest – it's not just the bloated Christmases, is it? It's every time you eat pizza or pasta or potatoes in pretty much any form to the point that you feel bloated, stuffed, unhealthy and often ashamed or guilty. It's every time you binge on cakes, or ice cream, or biscuits, or chocolate or all of the above and feel the same. It's not just once a year; it's pretty much day in day out, week in week out, month after month, year after year. From now on, you are not going to blindly follow convention to the detriment of your own happiness. You are going to be the one who controls what you eat, rather than the other way round. You will decide what your favourite foods are, you will decide how much you consume and you will decide how often.

Too good to be true? It's exactly what 99.99 per cent of creatures on this planet manage to do without thinking. Take a moment to look at all the benefits. In addition to the sheer pleasure of eating that you will experience, you will feel lighter, healthier, more energetic and self-confident and you will never again experience that horrible sense of guilt after finishing a meal. You'll be free from the eating binges that regularly punctuated your week. You'll be free from having to apply willpower in a constantly hopeless struggle to control the food that you eat.

You are not going on a diet, so you won't have to go through that soul-destroying process of counting calories. With this method there is no need to feel miserable about what you are about to do. The only reason anybody feels a sense of doom and gloom is because they remember the misery they've been through trying to diet. The fact that the diet did not work in solving their weight problem makes them feel like they've failed and they're afraid of failing again.

But diets are doomed to fail because they are asking you to do the impossible: to control what you eat through willpower for the rest of your life. Those people who appear to succeed with diets are merely applying more willpower, usually because their livelihood depends on it. Dancers, actors, jockeys, boxers, models – when their careers end, they tend to balloon in size. That is not success.

As long as you feel you are making a sacrifice you will never succeed in solving your problem permanently. Diets are all about restricting yourself. They involve giving up something that, up until now, you have considered a pleasure. Even if it's not actually doing you any good, the fact that you are depriving yourself of it will make you feel miserable. It will also make that particular item of food seem more precious: forbidden fruit.

The more precious the food becomes, the more deprived we feel because we can't have it. It is an ever-increasing cycle of misery that has to come to an end and, sure enough, sooner or later, our resistance gives out and we devour that precious taboo with a vengeance. We binge. And all that painful hard work is undone in an instant.

Restricting your eating also makes you feel permanently hungry. You become obsessed with the thought of your next meal, but when it comes it is a huge anticlimax. Compared to what you were used to eating, it is neither exciting nor enough and you're left feeling miserable again. There's a temptation to eat slightly more than the diet allows, which adds guilt to your misery.

Most people who attempt to lose weight through dieting actually gain weight in the long term. All it achieves is to make food appear more precious. And when you finally reach your target weight, what next? You abandon the diet and probably treat yourself to a little reward. In a fraction of the time it took you to lose the weight, you've put it all back on again and more.

Asking you to lose weight permanently by dieting is asking the impossible. So forget your feelings of failure over past diets that didn't work. The wonderful news is that it wasn't a weakness in you; it was a weakness in the method. With this method, you cannot fail, provided you follow all the instructions.

THIRD INSTRUCTION: START OFF WITH A FEELING OF EXCITEMENT AND ELATION

Forget about what's happened in the past, look to the future and cast off any sense of doom and gloom. Nothing bad is happening. On the contrary, you have every reason to feel elated. You are about to reverse a lifetime's brainwashing and achieve a sense of health and happiness greater than anything you have experienced before.

SUMMARY

- Your eating habits until now have not been controlled by you.
- What you think are your favourite foods are the product of conditioning since birth.
- You don't eat junk of your own free will; the food industry and your addiction drive you to it.
- Once you see the truth about the food you eat, you can never be fooled again.
- Diets don't work because they rely on willpower for life.
- Approach this method with a feeling of elation.

Chapter 4

THE TRAP

IN THIS CHAPTER

• *THE TWO ASPECTS OF ADDICTION* • *THE PITCHER PLANT*
• *NATURE'S WARNING LIGHT* • *AN INEVITABLE DECLINE*
• *THE MYTHS THAT KEEP YOU TRAPPED*

All addictions work in the same subtle and insidious way,
trapping you in a prison built by brainwashing.

When you eat or drink BAD SUGAR it passes rapidly into your
bloodstream, causing your blood sugar level to soar and then
crash. This crash manifests itself as a craving, a false hunger,
which you try to relieve with your "favourite food": more BAD
SUGAR. This is the cycle of addiction and it is the same with all
addictions: Each fix creates the craving for the next.

You might conclude, therefore, that if you can go long enough
without BAD SUGAR for all of it to pass out of your body, the
cravings should stop and your addiction will be cured. Yet we
know this is not the case. For smokers, alcoholics, heroin addicts
and overeaters alike, going "cold turkey" is not enough to fully cure
the addiction. Nicotine, for example, is purged from the body in a
matter of days, yet if all a smoker needed to do was stop smoking
for a week, the tobacco industry would have collapsed years ago.

The reason smokers continue to crave cigarettes long after all traces of nicotine have left their body is because addiction isn't just physical; it's mental too. In fact, 99 per cent of the problem is mental. The same is true of all addictions, including sugar. The problem lies in the belief that you derive some form of pleasure or crutch from eating sugary foods, or from processed or starchy carbohydrates. As long as you believe that, you will feel deprived and miserable if you can't have them.

We refer to the physical and mental aspects of addiction as two monsters: the Little Monster, which is the physical craving, and the Big Monster, which is the mental side. You can kill the Little Monster easily by going cold turkey, but if the Big Monster remains alive you will never be free.

The Big Monster is created by brainwashing. In the case of sugar addiction, it is the illusion that you gain some form of pleasure or crutch from eating BAD SUGAR foods. Because of the Big Monster, the addict seeks relief in the very thing that's causing the problem.

THE ILLUSION OF PLEASURE

The influence of the Big Monster becomes very clear when you look at an addiction like gambling, which has spread like wildfire in recent years. Gambling does not involve taking any substance, yet problem gamblers show all the same symptoms as other addicts. It is the illusion of pleasure that hooks them all.

When you have a craving for a cake or biscuit or some other so-called comfort food and you finally get your hands on one, how long does it take for the sense of relief to wash over you? It's instantaneous, isn't it? But it takes several minutes for that food to have a physical effect on your bloodstream, so how can that instant relief be due to the food?

It's not. The desire is caused by the belief that the sugary food is what you need and so as soon as you *think* you're getting it, the craving is relieved. It's not genuine pleasure; it is the illusion of pleasure.

HOW THE TRAP WORKS

You've probably come across the pitcher plant, that carnivorous funnel-shaped trap that lures flies into its digestive chamber with the sweet smell of nectar. The fly lands on the rim and begins to feed. The nectar seems like the best thing in the world, but it is the very thing that is luring the fly to its death. As it feeds, the fly slips unwittingly further and further towards the chamber until it falls right in and the plant consumes it.

The addiction trap works in a very similar way.

The difference between sugar addiction and other addictions is that we land on the rim of the pitcher plant before we are old enough to realize what we are doing. By the time we develop some awareness of the nutritional value of the foods we eat, we are well on our way down the slippery slope.

We are aware of all the arguments against sugary foods: the tooth decay, the weight gain and the increased risk of serious ailments like heart disease and Type 2 diabetes. We also know that gorging ourselves on these foods makes us feel lethargic, indulgent and ashamed. Yet we see millions of other people doing the same as us, many of them with no apparent ill effects at all, and at the same time we are bombarded with false information about how these foods will make us happy, cool, sexy…

So we close our eyes to the bad news and carry on consuming. Like the fly, we slip further and further down the slope. We think we're eating what we want to eat out of choice, but the truth is that, before we're even aware of what is good for us and what is not, **WE'VE ALREADY LOST CONTROL!**

As babies we're weaned on to jars of baby food which often contain sugar. Some only contain natural fruit sugars, but many have added sugar too. Many of the products that contain fruit sugar are also cause for concern, given that they are processed/blended, and therefore allow the sugar to be digested in "larger than natural quantities" at an unnatural speed. The items with added sugar are often packed full of it. The biggest-selling brand

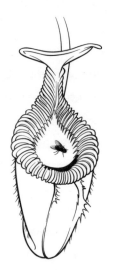

of rusks contain a massive 29g of sugar per 100g. It's not just baby foods; as we grow we're given starchy carbs (BAD SUGAR) as part of our daily intake – breakfast cereals, potato, rice, pasta and bread.

As children we are also given sweets, cakes, and biscuits only when our parents allow it. That may be all the time or it may be very seldom, but it is always someone else's decision. When we reach adulthood, we find we can decide for ourselves when we indulge in our favourite foods, and with the shackles off we tend to over-indulge. Don't mistake this for freedom of choice. In fact, it's the Big Monster that decides.

AN INEVITABLE DECLINE

The human body is an incredible machine with a remarkable ability to recover and adapt. Feed it poison and it will react violently to eject the poison from your system. That's why children are sometimes sick at birthday parties. All that sugary food gets expelled for their own good. But all the time that we are abusing our bodies we build a defensive tolerance to the poison, so that next time it takes more poison to create the same effect.

In other words, in order to get the same effect from the drug we need to increase the dose. That's why the tendency with any addiction is to take more, not less, which is what makes cutting down so hard. Remember, you are not trying to cut down; you are going to free yourself from the addiction altogether.

As time goes on and we slip further into the trap, taking bigger and bigger doses, the empty feeling after each fix also increases. On top of the physical low is a mental low caused by not being able to have the food you crave. It's a double low and the illusion of pleasure is magnified each time you relieve it. The "drug" becomes more precious, making the influence of the Big Monster more powerful.

The combined effect of the increase in both your tolerance and the empty feeling is that each fix never gets you quite back to your previous "high" and each low takes you lower than before.

HOW BAD SUGAR WORKS

The illusory boost that BAD SUGAR addicts get when they have BAD SUGAR is demonstrated by the graph below. By the time we're capable of conscious thought, we're already addicted to BAD SUGAR. Our blood sugar levels have been repeatedly corrupted over years, leaving us feeling dependent on it. It seems that we need BAD SUGAR in order to experience a normal level of wellbeing. It never occurs to us that we are perfectly equipped to handle the stresses, strains and demands of life without repeated doses of BAD SUGAR. We are fooled into believing that BAD SUGAR provides us with a boost.

The fact is that when we first consumed BAD SUGAR, we didn't experience any magical boost – certainly not one that we were conscious of, given that we were most likely in our cradles at the time. In fact it's quite

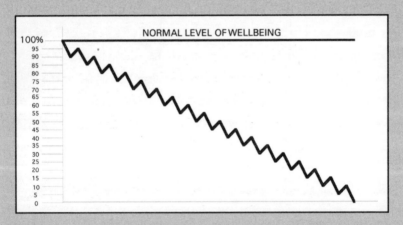

possible that we were caught in the BAD SUGAR trap before we were even born; we were subjected to the BAD SUGAR crashes caused by our mother's consumption during pregnancy. At some point following consumption, we experienced feelings of withdrawal: a mild, empty, insecure, feeling combined with a feeling of tiredness as our blood sugar levels crashed from a "false high". Again, we wouldn't have been conscious of this, although it may have contributed to our rate of kicking in the womb and, after birth, to the decibel level of our cries and an increased level of discomfort and irritability surrounding our subsequent demands for more food. Whether it was before birth – or afterwards – on the graph above we moved from the '100% normal level of wellbeing' (before we consumed BAD SUGAR) down to 90%.

When we consumed BAD SUGAR again, we received an apparent boost – not to 100% but to 95%. Once our natural hunger patterns are corrupted, continued consumption of BAD SUGAR leaves us incapable of returning to 100%. We do feel better than we did the moment before, yet all we've done is to have got rid of the unpleasant feeling that was created by BAD SUGAR in the first place. A lifetime's chain has started.

Soon the feeling of withdrawal returns and the mild, empty, insecure, tired feeling drags us back down to 85%. Each time we experience the sugar crash it sucks us deeper and deeper into the pit. We consume BAD SUGAR again and we immediately feel better than the moment before as we're boosted back up to 90%. The boost we receive never quite takes us back up to the previous "high". No matter how low BAD SUGAR drags us down, we remain foolishly grateful to it for the fake "high" it appears to produce.

Actually, the physical side (the Little Monster) is incredibly subtle and hardly noticeable. Hundreds of millions of babies have been born into BAD SUGAR addiction without their parents even noticing it. The real discomfort we experience in later life when we try to get off BAD SUGAR isn't caused by the physical effect itself, but by the feeling of deprivation we experience when we try to cut it out. Can you see how a lifetime of "fake highs" would have us convinced that there's nothing BAD about BAD SUGAR, in fact that everything about it is good? No wonder we find it hard to get out of the BAD SUGAR trap. It's this, added to the effect of the food companies advertising and marketing efforts, as well as society's misconceptions about the "benefits" of BAD SUGAR, that creates the brainwashing (the Big Monster) and causes the discomfort and feelings of deprivation.

Once you understand how you've been conned by BAD SUGAR, you'll find it not only easy to get free and stay free, but thoroughly enjoyable.

But you are not standing on a slippery slope like the fly. There is no physical force compelling you to eat BAD SUGAR. The trap is entirely in your mind. The fact that you are your own jailor is an ingenious aspect of the addiction trap, but it's also its fatal flaw. It means you have the power to escape whenever you choose, simply by understanding the nature of the trap and following a proven set of instructions to get free.

IF THE BRAIN CAN BE DECEIVED INTO BELIEVING THAT WE'RE GETTING PLEASURE OR A CRUTCH FROM THE FOOD WE EAT, DOES IT MATTER THAT IT ISN'T TRUE?

This is the misconception that stops us flying free: the myth that BAD SUGAR gives us some form of pleasure or crutch. If you were content with your eating habits, you wouldn't be reading this book. The fact is that while the Big Monster tells you that BAD SUGAR makes you happy, you know in your heart that the opposite is true. It's a kind of schizophrenia, a tug-of-war which you can only win by removing the brainwashing and killing the Big Monster.

While the brain may be deceived into thinking everything is all right, the opposite is true. You are risking your health and self-esteem, not to mention wasting your money and finding genuine happiness harder to come by. There's only so long you can go on burying your head in the sand.

SO WHAT'S STOPPING YOU?

The only way to reverse the inevitable decline is not simply to stop eating BAD SUGAR, but to unravel the brainwashing that makes you want to. There are two myths that stand in your way:

1. The myth that sugary or processed carb or starchy carb foods give you pleasure or a crutch.

2. The myth that escape will be hard.

You know now that any pleasure you perceive when eating BAD SUGAR is nothing more than an illusion. It is caused by the temporary and partial relief of a low, which was created by the last time you ate BAD SUGAR. It's important that you understand and accept this fact. If you go on believing that you get some sort of pleasure or crutch from eating BAD SUGAR, you will always feel deprived without it. You will also fear that life without sugar will be a life without happiness. In fact, the opposite is true: you will feel happier and healthier than you could believe when you cut BAD SUGAR out of your diet, but as long as you're in the trap it's difficult to see it.

The myth that escape from the trap will be hard is also perpetuated by the belief that you have some need or desire for sugary or processed or starchy carb foods and so giving them up will require tremendous willpower. This is reinforced by your own failed attempts to diet and the failed attempts of others. Despite summoning all your willpower, you were unable to succeed. But you know now that this was not your failure; it was the failure of the method you were following. Any method that relies on willpower is doomed to failure.

Let's be quite clear:

YOU ARE NOT 'GIVING UP' ANYTHING – IN FACT YOU'RE GETTING RID OF A DISEASE!

You are making marvellous gains. Life will be healthier and happier without sugar. You probably have good memories of times when you've consumed large quantities of BAD SUGAR food at parties. But where did the real pleasure come from? Was it really the food that made your day? Or was it the company, the conversation, the sheer pleasure of being with friends?

Take away the food and the situation would still have been enjoyable. Take away the company and the food would have been no fun. The fact is that it's not a case of avoiding food – it's a case of enjoying REAL food. Your enjoyment in the future will be heightened – not lessened. In addition to that, release from the feelings of guilt, remorse and the self-loathing of having over-indulged to the extreme is truly priceless.

If you've followed the second instruction and kept an open mind, you will see the truth in this argument. It's time to tackle the Big Monster, to unravel the brainwashing that has created your desire for BAD SUGAR.

SUMMARY

- Addiction is 1 per cent physical, 99 per cent mental.
- Addicts seek relief in the very thing that's causing the problem.
- The relief you feel is not the food; it's your desire for the food.
- With each "high" you fall a little further.
- The myths of "pleasure" and the "hardship of escape" keep you trapped.
- It's never too late to fly free.

Chapter 5

FIRST STEPS TO FREEDOM

IN THIS CHAPTER
•A NEW STATE OF MIND •A PERMANENT SOLUTION
•THE TUG-OF-WAR •SEEING THE REAL PICTURE
•THE TRUTH ABOUT SUGAR

Your escape from the sugar trap has already begun. Our job now is to remove the brainwashing that causes your desire for BAD SUGAR.

Everyone who picks up this book is eager to discover the secret of this magical cure and probably wonders why it isn't stated clearly in Chapter 1, but by now you should be able to see the two fallacies in this expectation:

1. It is not a secret.

2. There is no magic.

Easyway works by removing your desire for BAD SUGAR. It does this by applying undisputable logic to strip away the brainwashing that keeps you hooked, and replaces it with rational understanding.

This understanding is the key that will unlock your prison cell and it works like the combination lock of a safe. Each instruction must be understood and applied in order for the combination to work.

You have already been given the first three instructions:

1. FOLLOW ALL THE INSTRUCTIONS.

2. KEEP AN OPEN MIND.

3. START WITH A FEELING OF ELATION.

In getting this far, you have taken your first steps to freedom, but please be patient. The key to your escape does not lie in the final chapter or the first chapter, or any chapter alone; the whole book is the key and if you are to succeed in escaping the trap permanently, it is essential that you complete the programme.

EVER-PRESENT DANGER

Addicts are caught in a trap, just like someone who's stepped on a mantrap. Between us we have the two things we need to set them free: they contribute a strong desire to be released and Easyway has the key that will release them. All they have to do is follow the instructions.

However, once they are released, there is another danger: the trap still exists and we have to insure that they do not walk into it again.

A SOLUTION THAT LASTS FOREVER

The belief that sugar gives some form of pleasure or a crutch is so widely held that it would be unrealistic to expect you to reverse that bit of brainwashing immediately. People with addictions like drinking, smoking and gambling are notorious for "giving up" and starting again. That's because they rush into quitting through willpower alone without truly removing the desire.

People who go on diets are the same. They begin with a rush of enthusiasm, sparked by some new theory they've read about and fanned by their constant desire to lose weight, but all too soon the grim reality of the diet takes its toll on their enthusiasm and the desire for their "favourite foods", which never went away, takes over again.

As long as that desire remains, any attempt to escape from the trap will ultimately fail. You will be drawn back in.

So how do we remove the desire? Is it enough just to say sugar is bad for you and leave you to draw your own conclusions? If it was, we would all stop eating sugar at a young age. It is no secret that sugar is bad for us. We've been told so since we were children, despite being given it as a reward by the same people who warned us of its evils.

This method does not use shock tactics. You already know about the obesity, the growing risk of Type 2 diabetes and heart disease, not to mention the tooth decay; if this knowledge alone was enough to put you off, it would have done so by now. Smoking kills; it says so on the packet! Yet millions of people continue to smoke, despite being fully aware of the dangers.

When it comes to curing an addiction, shock tactics don't work. If they did Easyway would happily use them. But my aim is to set you free from slavery to sugar and to make sure you stay free. To do that I need to tackle the brainwashing that makes you believe that, despite all the associated health risks, there is something desirable about BAD SUGAR.

THE TUG-OF-WAR

All addicts are caught up in a tug-of-war. They say contradictory things like, "I know it's killing me, but I couldn't live without it." Or, "I know it's bad for me, but you've got to enjoy what you eat."

On the one side is the knowledge that the cigarette, the drink or, in this case, the BAD SUGAR is ruining their health, keeping them enslaved and making them miserable, but on the other side is the firm belief that life would not be worth living without it because it offers comfort, enjoyment and pleasure. They spend their lives wrestling with these contradictions, rather than getting on and enjoying themselves. They would be so much happier if they could win the tug-of-war.

The good news is that the tug-of-war actually becomes easy to win when you recognize that on the one side is fact – sugar does nothing for you whatsoever – and on the other side is myth – sugar gives you some sort of pleasure or crutch. All you have to do is see through the myth and the whole thing collapses.

You probably know people who, when the biscuits are passed round, are able to decline without any ceremony or fuss. They just don't seem to want one and they find it easy to refuse. For most of us who find it difficult not to eat the whole packet, let alone just the one, this can be hard to understand. How could anyone not be tempted by a biscuit?

Temptation only works if you have a desire for the thing that's being offered. And that's the fundamental difference between you and them. It's not that you eat biscuits and they don't; it's that they have absolutely no desire to do so.

They have been subjected to the same propaganda from the food industry and somewhere in their mind the seed will have been sown that sugar is a source of pleasure. But they also know that sugar is the cause of ill health and misery, and because they are not addicted they find it easy to win the tug-of-war.

Soon you will be one of them, though right now you may still find it hard to believe that you will ever be able to conquer your desire through reason.

EASYWAY DOES NOT REQUIRE THE POWER OF REASON TO OUTWEIGH DESIRE – IT REMOVES DESIRE ALTOGETHER

This is crucial. If you maintain a desire for BAD SUGAR you will suffer a feeling of deprivation when you stop and you will have to use willpower to fight it. As long as you rely on willpower, you will remain at risk of walking back into the trap for the rest of your life.

SEE THE REAL PICTURE

To get an idea of how your addiction looks through a non-addict's eyes, and how it will look to you once you're free, let's think about another addiction, hopefully one you don't suffer from: heroin. Heroin is such a dreadful addiction that most people never go near the drug. It is one that parents fear most for their children, a terrible, debilitating drug that turns the addict into a desperate, sick, terrified waif, often driven to crime to feed the addiction and, effectively, lost to those who love them.

It's easy for us to see the harm caused by heroin and to recognize the trap the addict is in, thinking that the next fix will make everything all right. If you can look at the heroin addict and see the mistake he's making, you are already on the way to solving your own problem. But you are in exactly the same trap as the heroin addict. The symptoms may not be as catastrophic… yet, it's worth bearing in mind that BAD SUGAR accounts for far more deaths than heroin. Your desire for BAD SUGAR is exactly the same as the junkie's misguided desire for heroin.

BAD SUGAR DOES NOT RELIEVE MISERY, IT CAUSES IT

It's essential to blow away these illusions once and for all, so that instead of seeing BAD SUGAR as a pleasure or crutch, you see the true picture. By the time you finish the book, your frame of mind will be such that, whenever you think about sugary, processed or starchy carb foods, instead of feeling deprived because you can no longer have them, you will feel overjoyed because…

YOU NO LONGER WANT THEM.

THE TRUTH ABOUT SUGAR

Refined sugar is known as an "empty carb" because it provides calories without any other nutritional value, such as vitamins, minerals and fibre. In other words, it is a pure hit of calories, and because of the absence of fibre to slow down digestion, it passes very quickly into the bloodstream.

This tidal wave of blood sugar causes a spike in the level of insulin you produce. Insulin is the hormone that regulates the level of glucose in the blood (blood sugar). It is produced in the liver and it performs a vital job, but the long-term effect of all these spikes is that your cells develop a resistance to the effect of insulin, with the result that they stop being receptive to the glucose they need. This condition is called Type 2 diabetes.

It's not just refined sugar in its crystalline or powdered form that has this effect. It exists in high quantities in many of the foods we eat and it's important that you are aware of what they are. You may have heard that certain foods, such as pasta, are good for getting energy before exercise. Pasta, rice, bread and other such foods are all empty carbs, offering little if any nutritional goodness. They do cause a sugar spike, driving up insulin levels, and the energy is also burned up very quickly, leaving a low, or "sugar crash". It's far better to get your energy from natural foods such as fruit and vegetables, which contain all the carbohydrate you need and deliver it more gradually, along with a wealth of other nutrients.

Most sugar addicts aren't interested in its nutritional value. They say it's the taste they can't resist. But just how great is the taste of sugar? Dip your finger in a bowl of sugar and see how it tastes. You'll feel the sweetness on your tongue, certainly, but what does it actually taste like?

If you really look for the flavour in sugary foods you will find that there's actually very little there. Think about pasta and rice: would you eat a plate of plain pasta or a bowl of plain rice? First of all you would add salt just to create some sensation on your taste buds, and then you would smother it in a well-seasoned sauce to give it flavour. What's the major ingredient in that sauce? Tomatoes and herbs. That's where the great taste comes from.

What about cakes and biscuits? When the manufacturers want them to taste of something, they add fruit jam, nuts or a fruit flavouring such as lemon. A biscuit or cake without any such addition is bland and has to be dunked in a hot drink to make it interesting.

In fact this is an important guiding factor. GOOD SUGAR foods can always be enjoyed raw and with nothing else added. Think of fruits – this applies to pretty much all of them: apples, oranges, blueberries, grapes, melon, blackcurrants, raspberries, strawberries, kiwi, bananas, pineapple, peaches, cherries, avocados, tomatoes, and so on. The same with vegetables: carrots, lettuce, celery, peppers, cucumber, cress, courgette, fennel, peas, onion, endless herbs, green beans, and so on.

If a fruit, or a variety of fruit, requires cooking or the addition of sugar in order to be palatable, the chances are that it's not something we should be eating. A naturally bitter or sour taste is Nature's warning to us to avoid it.

If a sugar food seems tasteless, unpalatable or unappealing raw, then your instinct alone should recognize it as dangerous.

Although a potato is a natural item, is it natural or good for us to eat? Think about it – it has to be cooked – often with the addition of butter or fat. You would never eat a raw potato out of choice. Isn't Nature trying to tell us something about that food? How about pasta? There's nothing natural about it and you would never eat pasta on its own out of choice. You would always add salt, mix it with butter, oil and/or sauces. Rice is the same. Bread? Well… how much bread could you eat without the addition of butter or other ingredients? Not much! It would be hard to force it down.

So BAD SUGAR food only seems to taste good or even be palatable when seasoning, fats, vegetables, fruit or nuts are added. Why not just eat the vegetables, fruit and nuts?

Another misconception among BAD SUGAR addicts is that it's cheap and convenient. With confectionery, you just grab it at the till, hand over some small change and you're on your way. It doesn't seem to dawn on them that the only reason they're at the till in the first place is because they want an excuse to buy confectionery. Addicts will make special journeys just to put themselves in the position where it looks like they're buying purely on impulse.

Two chocolate bars for a pound? Might as well – you can save one for later and then you're quids in. Of course, the second bar disappears soon after the first and you're left feeling greedy and ashamed. It's just another con trick from the food industry.

THEY'RE NOT INTERESTED IN YOUR CONVENIENCE; THEY'RE INTERESTED IN SELLING YOU SOME MORE BAD SUGAR!

Next time you're feeling peckish, stop and ask yourself, "Am

I really hungry or am I just being tempted by all the confectionery on display?" Confectionery offers empty calories and little, if any, nutritional value. If your hunger is genuine, an apple or banana will satisfy it and provide essential nutrition.

1. Fruit is cheaper than confectionery.
2. Fruit is more convenient than confectionery.
3. Fruit is incredibly good for you.

Fruit is a REAL convenience food. It comes ready to eat in its own natural packaging and any waste is biodegradable. Junk food isn't cheap. The deals that the supermarkets promote for their potato snacks, ready-made meals, cook-in sauces, and all kinds of other "foods" across the BAD SUGAR spectrum make it seem inexpensive. But when you consider the nutritional value contained in it, you're paying an awfully high price for very little.

When you start to question the myths about sugar, they quickly fall apart. Now I will look at how these myths become ingrained in our minds.

SUMMARY

- In order to free yourself permanently, you must remove the *desire* for BAD SUGAR.

- Winning the tug-of-war is easy when you stick to the facts.
- The sugar trap is the same as the heroin trap.
- See BAD SUGAR in its true light and you will begin to remove the desire.

Chapter 6

THE INCREDIBLE MACHINE

IN THIS CHAPTER
- *SECOND-HAND ADVICE* - *YOUR PRIDE AND JOY*
- *YOUR PERSONAL HANDBOOK* - *THE FLAW IN THE MACHINE*
- *THE FOURTH INSTRUCTION*

Mankind has achieved many great things, but these pale into insignificance next to the achievements of Nature.

Perhaps we should be proud of the advertising industry. After all, it is a testimony to our intellectual capacity to spread information. The imagination, creativity, design and execution of advertising campaigns are all evidence of the incredible intellect that sets us apart from the rest of the animal kingdom.

However, advertising is also a prime example of mankind's fundamental weakness: the capacity to spread and believe MISINFORMATION.

The advertising industry has been spreading misinformation about sugar for years, using every trick it could concoct to brainwash us into believing that sugar can enhance our life. But advertising isn't the only culprit. Our parents play an unwitting part in the brainwashing too, telling us we can have sweets as a treat if we're good, rather than warning us off them altogether, as they would with a drug like heroin. Even the medical profession adds to the confusion, putting out information that seems to contradict itself every few years and, until recently, using huge amounts of BAD SUGAR in many medicines. Until very recently (and in some cases even today) large parts of the medical profession still recommend that sufferers of Type 2 diabetes eat starchy carbs with every meal; this is like pouring petrol on to a house fire instead of water.

The pharmaceutical industry makes money out of their "medicines" which are taken by the sufferer for the duration of their entire lives, and the BAD SUGAR industry keeps selling its poison – supported by the medical profession!!

Extraordinary as it may seem, the current global Type 2 diabetes epidemic could not just be halted in its tracks, but also be reversed, purely by having most sufferers cut out BAD SUGAR: cost to the sufferer – nil; cost to the health service – nil; cost to the pharmaceutical and BAD SUGAR industry – HUGE!

The advertising industry has a vested interest in keeping us hooked on BAD SUGAR, but even those with good intentions cannot be relied upon to give us the information we need. They take their knowledge from other people, who have in turn taken it from equally unreliable sources. It's a case of the blind leading the blind.

YOUR PRIDE AND JOY

If you had a problem with your car, who would you turn to for advice: a man in the pub or the car manufacturer? The car is one of the most complex and impressive machines mankind has ever devised. It fulfils numerous functions all at once and is powered by a carefully co-ordinated sequence of compressions and explosions, all going on beneath the bonnet while you glide along in serene comfort inside.

Most of us know very little about how our car actually functions; all we care about is that it does. In order to ensure that it continues to do so, we play our part by filling it with the right fuel and making sure it gets regularly cared for by an expert. Listening to second-hand advice about what may or may not be a problem with the engine is only going to lead to one thing:

BREAKDOWN!

To some people, the car is the pinnacle of human invention, their pride and joy; yet we all possess a far more complex and ingenious machine: the human body.

There are several similarities between your body and a car: they both have mechanical parts; they both need fuel and air to keep them functioning; they both need to be maintained. But compared to your body, the car is about as sophisticated as an old-fashioned typewriter is in comparison with a modern laptop.

Your body is capable of performing a multitude of functions all at once, in perfect co-ordination, without you even being aware of it. Your heart pumps vital supplies to every corner of your body; your lungs extract oxygen from the air you breathe; your digestive system sorts all the nutrients from the food you eat and sends them to where they're needed and your immune system fights off infection and repairs injuries.

All this happens simultaneously and, for the most part, without a hitch. And because it happens without any conscious effort on your part, you take it for granted. You don't have to know how it functions to keep it working for year upon year, all you have to do is keep it fuelled and cared for.

But there is one important difference between your body and your car: man invented the car and is, therefore, the leading authority on how it works. There is no more reliable source of information on how to maintain it than the manufacturer that made it, so it makes good sense to consult the manufacturer's guide.

Your body was neither invented nor constructed by man. It is infinitely more complex and ingenious than any man-made machine and it is infinitely more precious. So why do we listen to second-hand advice about how to keep it in good working order?

The usual answer to this question is, "Because we don't get born with a handbook." But the fact is we do: Nature's Guide.

The same ingenious force that created the human body, whatever you may believe that to be, also gave us instincts, which enabled us to survive and become the dominant species on the planet long before the arrival of modern medicine, the microwave and the nutritionist. Our ancestors didn't need to be told about calories and vitamins, any more than you need to know about the internal workings of your car's engine to enjoy a ride in the country. Nature's Guide told them what fuel to put in and what to avoid.

WHERE OUR INTELLIGENCE HAS GOT US

The second instruction was to keep an open mind. It's important that you follow this instruction because, as intelligent beings, we tend to be closed to the idea of following instinct in preference to intellect.

Say you had to gamble all your possessions on the outcome of a football match. You can seek the advice of two people: one of them is the most intelligent person on the planet, who has predicted the result of a hundred matches and achieved a 75 per cent success rate; the other is an illiterate yokel who has made a million predictions and got them all correct. Who would you trust?

Because we don't understand our instincts, we regard them as hit or miss – nothing more than guesswork. But instinct is not hit or miss, it is the result of three million years of trial and error. It is what enables wild animals to breed and to feed without eating anything harmful to them.

The power of intellect over instinct is what has given us dominion over the rest of the animal kingdom, so you might conclude that intellect should be our guiding light. But there are enough stark examples of intellect backfiring on us to make you think again, i.e. war, pollution and genocide, to name but three. Clearly intellect is not always a force for good.

Medical science has made some spectacular discoveries and found ingenious ways to alleviate illnesses and even reconstruct parts of the human body, yet at the same time it has made us susceptible to conditions that didn't exist before. It brings to mind John Steinbeck's classic novel *Of Mice and Men* and the simple character Lennie, who was so grateful to his companion George for saving him from drowning that he forgot it was George who had pushed him in in the first place!

Modern medicine, for all its cures, can often make us weaker, not stronger.

THE BUCKET

We go through life accepting all manner of ailments as normal. Headache, indigestion, constipation, diarrhoea... we take our medicine and, if we're lucky, the symptoms disappear. But we're not surprised when they return. We resign ourselves to suffering on a regular basis.

With any other problem in life, we try to establish the cause and fix it once and for all. If you have a leak in your roof you can do one of two things: you can put a bucket underneath to catch the drips, or you can mend the roof and stop the water coming in. The bucket may be the quick and easy option, but who wants a bucket as a permanent feature in their house, and what happens when you want to go on holiday?

When you go to the doctor with a pain of some kind and he gives you a prescription for a drug to take the pain away, you are effectively trying to solve the problem of a leaky roof by putting a bucket under it. Are you going to keep taking those drugs for life? In America, the frontier of modern medicine, half the population take prescription drugs every month! Clearly modern medicine is not enabling us to stand on our own two feet.

Take a condition like indigestion. Perhaps you suffer from it.

It can be very uncomfortable and will make you want something to take the pain away fast. But the pain is serving a purpose: it is a warning sign that something is wrong. There are three things you can do: 1. Take a painkiller; 2. Take something to quell the indigestion; 3. Find the cause of the indigestion and fix it.

Let's go back to the oil warning light in your car. That light is designed to make you react. Like pain, it is there to nag you until you do something about it. If you want to stop the nagging you have three choices: 1. Remove the bulb; 2. Top the engine up with oil; 3. Find out why the oil is low and fix it.

Option 1 will stop the warning light nagging you, but pretty soon your engine will seize. Option 2 will stop the light from nagging you temporarily until the oil runs low again. Option 3 will solve the whole problem and give you peace of mind.

Now apply that thinking to your indigestion. A doctor will offer you options 1 and 2. The focus of modern medicine is on the symptoms not the cause. Drug companies make a fortune selling us pain relief and remedies for ailments that are actually caused by poor diet. As a result, more and more people are rattling around on medication, reducing their body's ability to put up its own defences and perpetuating the damage being caused by an unhealthy diet.

If you keep using indigestion remedies, guess what? You're eating the wrong kind of foods. The solution isn't to keep taking the remedies, it's to find out what foods are causing the problem and to eliminate them from your diet.

The fabulous news is that normally the foods that cause this kind of issue are addictive BAD SUGAR foods. Once you've got rid of them from your diet, you cease to be addicted and it becomes easy and enjoyable to avoid them.

NATURE'S WARNING SIGNS

Indigestion, constipation, diarrhoea, headaches etc are all warning signs in Nature's Guide. Treat them with a "magic pill" that stops your brain from registering the symptom and you are merely removing the bulb. Some symptoms, such as vomiting or coughing, are also part of the cure: Nature's method of ejecting alien matter from the stomach or lungs. Take a pill to prevent those symptoms and you are actively hindering the cure.

Many of the medicines that doctors prescribe actually make the problem worse. Drugs like Valium and Librium have been found to cause problems rather than alleviate them. Drugs are poisons administered in controlled doses. The body will react against the poison, building immunity to it. As a result, stronger and stronger doses of the drug will be required in order to overcome the body's natural reaction, until it no longer has any effect at all. The original problem has not been eradicated, and now the patient finds that they are also addicted to the painkillers.

Nature has provided us with our own protection from disease, the immune system. Drugs destroy the immune system. Wild animals rarely die from disease. When they do, it is usually due to pollution caused by humans. It is also very rare for them to be killed by their own kind. It is only intelligent man that dies mainly from disease or violence from our own species. By allowing our intelligence to act against Nature, we have put evolution into reverse.

THE FLAW IN THE MACHINE

The human being is an incredible machine, yet there is a flaw that has caused us untold misery.

Animals avoid many of the problems that afflict mankind because they lead their lives by instinct. We also have the ability to live by instinct, but our intellect gets in the way. That is the flaw in the incredible machine. Our unique asset is also our unique undoing.

Nature has given us a tool to gain power over the rest of the animals, but we misuse it. We think we can outsmart Nature itself. When our instinct and intellect are in conflict, we find it easier to make a reasoned argument in support of the intelligent course of action, even when there is overwhelming evidence to the contrary. We talk about the miracle of childbirth. The reason it appears to be a miracle is because the reproduction of life is way beyond the capacity of our intelligence.

It is not our fault that we are flawed in this way and it needn't be a problem, provided we can open our minds and recognize that we are. If you can see that, you will also see that Nature, not man, is the leading authority on how your body works and if you want to know how best to maintain it, the best source to turn to is Nature's Guide – instinct.

FOURTH INSTRUCTION: IGNORE ANY ADVICE THAT GOES AGAINST NATURE'S GUIDE

Now that we have established the authority of Nature's Guide, we can begin to look more closely at the advice it offers. Like the rest of the animal kingdom, you will be able to eat as much of your favourite foods as you want, when you want and be able to maintain excellent health naturally and effortlessly.

SUMMARY

- Your body is infinitely more complex than your car.
- Man designed the car; he didn't design man.
- The leading authority on how your body works is Nature's Guide.
- Trusting intelligence over instinct has brought us untold misery.
- Ignore any advice that goes against your instinct.

CHAPTER 7

HOW WE LOST SIGHT OF NATURE'S GUIDE

IN THIS CHAPTER
•ACQUIRED TASTE •WHY WE JUMP THE WARNING LIGHTS
•KNOWING WHO TO TRUST •THE FIFTH INSTRUCTION
•MAKING PROGRESS

While our interest in second-rate foods was born out of necessity, our dependence upon them is something we have the power to change.

Have you ever wondered why a child can get sick at a birthday party? All those fries, pizza, cake, all those biscuits and sweets, all those sugary drinks – they overdo it in their excitement and they just can't keep it down. But have you ever thought about the physical effect that causes them to be sick?

There are two points to observe here:

1. Children do not naturally self-regulate when faced with an abundance of sugary food;

2. They sometimes don't just feel a bit poorly after eating it; they actually bring the food back up.

The first point is evidence that refined sugar does nothing for you at all. It provides no satisfaction because it contains none of the nutrients your body needs. So a child will keep eating until they are over-full because the gauge that tells them they have satisfied their hunger records no nutritional intake. I will look more closely at hunger later.

The second point is evidence of another ingenious function of the incredible machine. When the body detects poison, it does everything it can to expel it from your system. If you've ever experienced vomiting to the point where you feel there is nothing left to come up, you will know just how vigorous your body can be in clearing out poison. It's unpleasant and upsetting, but it's a life-saver.

So why aren't we always sick whenever we eat BAD SUGAR? Here again is another marvel of the incredible machine. While it is finely attuned to the food we eat, your body is also very resilient, far more so than your car. Put diesel in a petrol engine and you'll be lucky if it ever works again. At the very least, you will have a very expensive repair on your hands. But when you eat the wrong foods, your body does its best to absorb the impact, even to the extent of developing an immunity to the poison.

This is one of the amazing attributes of the human body, but it should not be taken for granted. Your body's capacity to roll with the punches is not infinite and while there may be no physical signs of damage on the outside, we already know that the damage on the inside can be severe. The body's resilience, coupled with brainwashing from the food industry, has led us to believe we can get away with eating just about anything, to the point that we don't really even question the intake of these foods any more. But the statistics on obesity, diabetes, heart disease and other ailments prove the opposite is true.

ACQUIRING AND UNACQUIRING TASTE

Your body's ability to adapt to foods that it wasn't designed to eat is also part of our survival story. While Nature's Guide ensured that we were drawn to the foods that were best for us by making them taste the best, it would have been a short-lived plan if there had been no contingency for when these foods were not available. The contingency was to give us the ability to acquire a taste for second- and third-rate foods, so that we could continue to eat and avoid starvation when our favourite foods were scarce.

Our ancestors also knew the importance of storing food for times of shortage and, being the most intelligent species on the planet, they developed the most ingenious methods for doing so. But they will have quickly discovered the drawback with food that gets left uneaten: it goes off. In fact, it gets eaten by other creatures, namely bacteria.

Bacteria are just as much a part of Nature's Guide as we are. They just happen to like the same foods as we do. So our ancestors had to find a way to preserve their food against decay, and over time they came up with a range of methods, such as cooking, smoking, salting, freezing, pickling, bottling, canning and refining. In every case they were effectively making the food inedible to bacteria. But in so doing they were also taking out most of the properties that made it food in the first place – the nutrients.

> **How sugar preserves**
>
> Sugar is a very effective preservative. It works by drawing water out of the food or tying it up in the food so that it is not available to bacteria. It also drives the water out of the bacteria themselves, preventing them from growing.

Preserving food in this way was a necessary adaptation for our ancestors, a way of ensuring survival when the supply of favourite foods dried up. It was used to sustain sailors on long voyages, but they suffered as a consequence, with diseases such as rickets and scurvy, due to the lack of nutrients. Fresh fruit was a godsend on sea voyages.

There was no confusion then as to which were the right foods to eat, but as the Industrial Revolution drew people out of the country and into the towns, it became increasingly difficult to provide enough fresh food for everybody and so the demand for processed food exploded. The provision of processed foods became big business and once that happened, we were all at the mercy of commerce.

Today, we are utterly dependent on supermarkets. They sell us frozen foods, which we take home and put in our freezers, or dried goods, which we store in our cupboards for months, even years. We are told that these foods are of genuine nutritional benefit. We are even led to believe that we need them to survive. Who are we to question it? After all, we've been sold the same line from infancy, even by our own parents.

Love kills

There is a terrific responsibility on parents to safeguard their children's health through the food they feed them. Sadly, parents take their guidance from unreliable sources. As a result, children are routinely encouraged to try foods that trigger a warning light, and in some cases punished if they don't. They are similarly encouraged to finish everything on their plate, regardless of how hungry they are. Most parents regard it as their duty to instil these habits in their children, believing that they will help them to enjoy a more varied and interesting diet in adult life, and to be strong and healthy.

Children who refuse to eat so-called grown-up foods are labelled as fussy, but all they are doing is responding to Nature's Guide. If they were allowed to eat only what appeals to their instincts, they would avoid getting hooked on many of the processed foods that we then try to cut out later in life when weight problems and eating disorders catch up with us.

The fact is that by the time the child is capable of independent thought, they are already addicted to junk and therefore often fooled into making bad food decisions. Even so, with young enough children, put a bowl of fresh fruit next to a bowl of sweets and it's normally the fresh fruit that disappears first.

Parents who read this book have a marvellous

opportunity not only to solve their own eating problems, but also to ensure that their children do not suffer in later life. Question the brainwashing that you were brought up with and instead apply the common-sense guide that Nature has provided to your children.

Nature did not intend for us to carry on eating inferior foods when our favourite foods became available again, yet this is exactly what we have done. We have conditioned ourselves to regard foods that are bad for us as favourites.

Taste is a personal thing. Ask a room full of people what they think of paté. Some will say it tastes revolting; others will say it tastes divine.

How can the same food provoke such polarized responses? Because taste is acquired by each one of us individually and it differs according to the way we've been conditioned.

As any Italian will tell you, nothing beats the taste of Mama's cooking. You don't have to be Italian to go along with that. Those favourite dishes that our mothers (or fathers) made for us when we were growing up are seldom matched by anyone else's recipes later in life. Why do you think that is?

The reason some foods, such as chocolate, are more universally popular than others, such as paté, is purely because more of us have been conditioned to like chocolate than have been conditioned to like paté. The only foods that taste good to everybody are those we are drawn to by Nature's Guide.

The belief that sugary foods taste good is an illusion brought about by conditioning. If you believe it's an inherent quality in the food, why does your own personal taste alter during the course of your life?

As children, we devour jelly and ice cream with a passion. At parties it is the special treat that is kept until last, after we've eaten the sandwiches, fries and pizza. By the time it is served our anticipation is at fever pitch and if someone promised us a lifetime's supply of the stuff we would jump at it.

Yet offer an 18-year-old jelly and ice cream and they'll think you're being funny. By that age, the idea of it being a special treat has long since worn off and there is no desire for it whatsoever. You've moved on to more grown-up poisons, like alcohol or coffee or more sophisticated desserts. If a child tastes alcohol, they'll recoil in disgust. Yet by the time we're 18, we have usually got over that reaction.

Acquiring a taste for any food means overriding a warning light. The gag reflex a child displays when they taste alcohol is purely instinctive.

Your senses detect poison and trigger a physical response to reject it. But your body is adaptable and if you persist with the same poison, it will try to override the warning light.

There is a theory that if you sample any food 14 times, you will acquire a taste for it. What you are actually doing is acquiring a loss of taste. The body builds an immunity, suppressing the senses that trigger the reflex to reject it. Through forcing your body to adapt, you destroy part of its ability to protect you.

Why would intelligent man do such a thing to himself? Because the instinctive messages we receive from our senses have been confused by the misinformation we've received from all those outside influences who tell us they know best. We are told that drinking alcohol is a grown-up thing to do and at 18 there is nothing we want more than to be thought of as grown-up. We persevere through the revulsion, the nausea and the hangovers until we find we can drink without feeling sick.

Similarly, eating a wide variety of foods is regarded as grown-up. Children can be picky, but in an adult it's not a trait that's admired. So we force ourselves to "acquire a taste" for all sorts of things that as children we find repugnant: oysters, blue cheese, beer and alcohol, coffee, etc.

Without the brainwashing we could and would live very happily without these items. We would also consume a lot less BAD SUGAR. Why? Because sugar is the food industry's way of making second- and third-rate foods seem palatable.

Remember, refined sugar is designed to replicate the sweetness of our favourite foods. Nature gave us the ability to adapt to second-rate foods when our favourites were scarce; it didn't intend us to go on eating them when our favourite food became available again. Yet that is what we've done. Thanks to refined sugar, we have come to regard eating junk as natural.

FIFTH INSTRUCTION: FREE YOURSELF FROM SLAVERY TO YOUR PRESENT TASTES AND EATING HABITS

You might think that if the brainwashing has been going on for so many years, it will take a mighty effort to get free. And if we have become so incapable of recognizing Nature's Guide, how will you ever be able to identify the foods that really do taste the best?

The good news is that, just as your body has the incredible power to adapt, its resilience also makes it a fast healer. Your natural instinct is still very much intact and you can quickly restore its power over the brainwashing just by following the instructions in this book.

If you try to solve your sugar addiction without undoing the brainwashing, by relying on willpower, it will take a mighty effort and you will most probably fail. The beauty of this method is that it is easy. All you have to do is follow the instructions.

Just as you can learn to "enjoy" the taste of any food by eating it regularly enough, you can learn to dislike them again too and rediscover the pleasure in eating the foods that are good for you.

WHO'S BRAINWASHING WHOM?

Taste can be acquired and unacquired very quickly. Whatever we decide we want to eat, we can adapt accordingly in a short space of time. So it all comes down to how you decide what you want to eat.

This raises a very important question and it's one you may be wanting to ask. Up until now you've been following the instructions and keeping an open mind to everything you've read. But keeping an open mind means questioning both sides of the argument. Until you complete the book and are convinced that everything I've told you is true, I want you to accept the possibility that it could be true, but I don't want you to accept it blindly. Question both sides of the argument. That is the only way to come to the truth.

How can you be sure that it's not Easyway that's doing the brainwashing? Perhaps the basis of this method is to brainwash you into believing that the foods you've regarded as your favourites until now actually taste bad, and that the foods that are best for you also taste the best?

Well, if that were the case, would it not be preferable to the alternative? If this book could brainwash you into liking only foods that were good for you, it would achieve its aim of putting the joy back into eating. But that is not how the method works and to prove it, here's another illusion.

Look closely. What do you think this says?

Now hold the book a little further away. What do you see? Some people see the word "Good" first and then "Evil" later. Others see it the other way round. It doesn't matter. The point is that once you see the full picture, you can never be fooled by half of it.

The brainwashing of the food industry has offered you only one point of view: it has convinced you that BAD SUGAR gives you some sort of pleasure or crutch. You know it's making you miserable but you are convinced that there must be something good about it to make you keep coming back for more. But what if there wasn't? Think back to the heroin addict. What if the only thing that kept you coming back for more was addiction?

The aim of this method is to show you that there is an alternative view: that sugar does absolutely nothing for you whatsoever. It doesn't do this through brainwashing; it does it by stripping away the misinformation that has blinded you to the truth. It's actually COUNTER-BRAINWASHING! Once you can see through the illusion, you can never be taken in by it again.

A TALL TALE

This method enables you to see through the illusions by presenting you with undeniable facts. For example, we are told that we need to eat meat to get protein to make us big and strong, and dairy for calcium to give us healthy teeth and bones. We grow up believing this to be true.

We are one of many land mammals occupying the planet, all of different shapes and sizes, some of which eat meat, some of which don't. The largest of all land mammals is the elephant. It must consume some protein and calcium to grow to that size and sport such magnificent tusks, right? But the elephant doesn't eat meat, nor does it eat dairy.

The fact is we can get all the protein, calcium and

other nutrients we need from our favourite foods as designed by Nature's Guide, without eating meat or dairy. When presented with facts like this, you start to question everything else you've ever been told about nutrition.

Now don't panic! I'm not about to suggest that you become vegetarian and avoid dairy products – although if you did so, you'd probably become infinitely healthier. Our objective is to free you from your addiction to BAD SUGAR, but I just want you to think about Nature's Guide for a while.

Think about strong, muscular, powerful, fast animals: lions, tigers, jaguars, cheetahs, bulls, wolves, bears, rhinos and so on. They all have one thing in common; they don't drink milk beyond infancy and they don't eat BAD SUGAR.

How do you think these supreme beasts would look and behave if they were fed bowls of pasta, rice, or fed plates of pizza, or troughs of fried or roast potatotes, sweets and chocolate? Do you think it would make them strong? Or do you think it would make them slow, sick and susceptible to illness?

You might think that the idea of feeding those incredible animals those foods is ridiculous, but how much more ridiculous is it to have bombarded your strong healthy body with those foods for your entire life? How much more ridiculous is it to have nurtured and raised your children to consider those foods precious and desirable? Don't beat yourself up about this – you took a wrong turn, that's all. When you realize you've walked into a blind canyon, the only sensible thing to do is turn around and walk your way back out.

Our real favourite foods are a matter of fact. Their taste is not acquired, it is enjoyable from the very first time we try them and they never stop tasting good. But the culmination of addiction since infancy, years of misinformation and powerful suggestion from food advertisers, has rendered our instinct for our real favourite foods ineffective. We no longer follow Nature's Guide because our heads are full of a confusing mass of mixed messages.

MAKING REAL PROGRESS

We are conditioned to regard any transition from old to new as progress, but the way our eating habits have changed over the past few hundred years is not progress, it is a backwards step. Only now that the world is waking up to the damage caused by BAD SUGAR are we beginning to open our minds to this fact. For centuries, we have accepted the word of the food industry and taken its processed products as part of the advancement of our species. Now we know different. It's time to revert to Nature's Guide – that will be real progress. When you started reading this book, you probably found it hard to believe that you could eat as much of your favourite foods as you wanted, when you wanted and be free from BAD SUGAR. Just like the Good/Evil illusion, you should now be able to see that this is possible. In fact, it isn't just possible, it's natural. It's exactly what 99.9 per cent of the animal kingdom do all the time.

If you are still unsure, please go back and read this chapter again. It is important to remove preconceptions about what your favourite foods are and open your mind to the possibility that pretty much everything you have believed until now is a myth. This realization should fill you with joy. It is the beginning of the unravelling of the brainwashing that has kept you trapped.

Remember the aim of this book is to help you enjoy and feel happy about the food you eat. It is not to make you feel deprived. You are not giving up anything, only making marvellous gains. You have everything to look forward to and nothing to fear. Keep following the instructions and your escape will be easy.

SUMMARY

- **Your body is designed to reject poison, but it will build a tolerance when required.**

- **We develop a taste for second-rate foods as Nature's way of ensuring we survive when our favourite foods are scarce.**

- **An acquired taste is actually an acquired loss of taste. We can "unacquire" a taste just as easily.**

- **Social conditioning forces us to acquire a taste for poisons.**

- **Free yourself from slavery to your present tastes and eating habits.**

- **When you see the full picture you can never be fooled by half of it.**

- **You are not giving up anything.**

Chapter 8

FUELLING UP AND BURNING OFF

IN THIS CHAPTER
• *SELF-IMAGE* • *WHY YOU PUT ON WEIGHT*
• *EXERCISING TO LOSE WEIGHT* • *WHY WE EAT*
• *HOW TO SATISFY HUNGER*

The balance between intake and disposal is fundamental to your physical condition. Put BAD SUGAR into your system and you will always struggle to get the balance right.

Another trait that is uniquely human is the tendency to judge our fitness by our weight. If we're feeling out of shape, we look in the mirror and say, "I must do something about my weight." As a result, weight becomes the chief motivator behind our attempts to get fit. We decide that we need to lose X number of pounds or kilograms and then embark on a regime of diet, exercise, or both, in the hope of achieving that.

You may argue that weight is the only visible proof that you are getting fitter, but is that really the case? Is it the figure on the scales that makes you miserable when you feel you've overeaten, or is it the way you look and feel? And how do you know what your ideal weight should be? Everybody is different.

There's an exercise we like to do at the Easyway clinics, which always prompts an interesting response. Take the fastest man on Earth – for the last few years it's been Usain Bolt, the phenomenal Jamaican sprinter. What do you think Usain Bolt weighs? The estimates we get vary by as much as fifty pounds.

When we're asked to reveal the answer, we have to shrug and say we have no idea. Why do we need to know? You only have to look at Usain Bolt to see he's in superb physical condition. If you were in similar condition, would you care how much you weighed?

It is not your scales that will tell you when you are the exact weight you want to be; it is your eyes and your lungs. When you like what you see in the mirror and can carry out your day-to-day activities without getting out of breath, you will know that you have achieved your ideal weight. You won't need scales to confirm the fact; you will just feel it. And it is a very good feeling.

If you set yourself a target weight you are letting the tail wag the dog and putting obstacles in your way. Don't rely on your scales to tell you when you're happy. Who knows what your target weight is? Estimates for Usain Bolt's vary by fifty pounds! You might find you reach a condition you're happy with before you get down to your target weight. What then? Do you have to keep losing weight before you allow yourself to be happy?

Anyway, the objective of this book is to free you from your addiction to BAD SUGAR. That's all that counts. As a wonderful bonus of achieving that, you'll be healthier, fitter and find it easy to lose weight and to look exactly the way you want to look.

SIXTH INSTRUCTION: DISREGARD ANY PRECONCEIVED TARGET WEIGHT

WHY DO WE PUT ON WEIGHT?

It seems a simple question, but it's one we often ask ourselves in exasperation. You've tried the diets, you've put yourself through exercise regimes, yet the pounds keep piling on. Why?

Let's begin with the simple answer.

YOU GAIN WEIGHT IF YOU ADD MORE THAN YOU TAKE AWAY

In other words, if your intake exceeds your output, you will put on weight. Some people try to muddy the waters by citing glandular problems or a slow metabolism. These may have a bearing on intake and disposal, but the basic fact remains: if you consume more than you burn off or pass out as waste, you will gain weight.

So there are two sides to the equation: intake and output. In order to balance the equation you simply have to adjust one or the other, or both.

This is not news: everybody knows there are two ways to lose weight: diet and exercise. No doubt you have tried one or the other and probably both. So why are you reading this book? Clearly neither worked for you. The fact is both of them are missing the point.

BURNING OFF

Lack of exercise is frequently cited as the main reason people become overweight. Obese people are generally regarded as lazy, while sportspeople, dancers and others who make a career out of vigorous exercise certainly give the impression that weight is not a problem for them. But just because they manage to control their weight, doesn't mean they don't crave junk food just as much, if not more, than you do.

The developed world has become obsessed with exercise, most of which takes place without actually going anywhere, on rowing machines, treadmills, exercise bikes, cross-trainers and other such devices, yet we are witnessing an obesity epidemic. The claim that special exercise is essential to weight loss is a smokescreen that gives us an excuse to carry on eating junk.

What happens when you exercise? Yes, you burn off more calories, but you also become more hungry, so you eat more. And because you feel you've worked hard, you allow yourself a reward – you blow out on junk.

The only "reward" is a persistent weight problem.

If good physical condition was dependent on vigorous exercise, wouldn't cats be tremendously fat? OK, some are when overfed by their owners, but the average cat will leap up on to a six-foot fence and walk along it without any loss of balance, despite the fact that it spends most of its life asleep! Consider the big cats in the wild; have you ever seen one that looks out of shape? Yet they don't spend hours every day charging about in order to maintain their figure, they expend energy when they need to, to hunt or to flee, and spend the rest of the time lying down.

How do they do it? By making sure their intake is balanced with their output.

Please be clear, this is not to say that an active lifestyle is not a good thing. Exercise is wonderful when pursued for pleasure. A round of golf, a game of tennis, a walk in beautiful scenery, taking a refreshing stroll rather than taking the bus for the whole journey... If you get genuine pleasure from a treadmill, then do it for that reason. But exercising in order to lose weight is as futile as taking your car for a drive just to reduce the weight in the petrol tank.

REDUCING THE INTAKE

So we turn our attention to the other side of the equation: intake. If exercise isn't the answer then it has to come down to reducing the amount you eat. But wait, we've said all along that diets don't work. That's right, because diets require you to make a sacrifice, which in turn requires willpower. You can will yourself to follow the diet for a certain amount of time, maybe even until you reach your target weight, but the feeling of deprivation will be nagging away at you the whole time, and as soon as you achieve your goal, as dictated by the scales, you will allow your willpower to give in. Diets always end with a return to the way you ate before and it's heartbreaking how quickly the weight goes back on.

So if diets don't work and neither does exercise, what is the answer? Well, we're two-thirds of the way there. Controlling your intake is the only way to achieve and maintain your ideal weight, but dieting is not the way to do it. What's the point of going through misery and deprivation? The good things in life don't have to come through hardship. You can eat as much as you want; you just need to make sure that it's the right type of food! It's not so much about avoiding calories; it's about avoiding the empty ones.

WHY WE EAT

Let's try another apparently simple question: why do we eat?

The simple answer would be, "To avoid dying". But is that really why you eat? Every time you sit down to a meal, are you thinking, "I need to do this otherwise I'll starve to death"?

We use expressions like "I'm starving" or "I'm famished", but we don't know what starvation feels like. It's more likely that we don't even think about our reasons for eating when we sit down to a meal. If asked we'd say, "It's what I do at this time of day."

Routine is a big factor in when and how we eat. There are other factors too, such as reward or comfort. The snacks you eat between meals could be part of your daily routine, or they could be a little treat for yourself.

Sometimes we eat to take our mind off more mundane issues. You're sitting at your desk trying to finish a piece of work that is becoming a drag. It's taking longer than you expected and you're losing confidence in your ability to finish it satisfactorily. You want some relief. So you reach for the biscuits or sweets or a chocolate bar.

Smokers reach for a cigarette in the same circumstances, for the same reason. They believe the cigarette will give them some relief from the stress they're feeling. But soon you have to return to your work and the problem is still there. The food or the cigarette hasn't relieved it at all. Let's face it; it's ridiculous to think it would.

Boredom, comfort, reward, routine may be the reasons we give for eating, but are they the real reasons Nature gave us to make sure we maintain a proper intake of nutrition?

When we eat as Nature intended, it doesn't just prevent us from dying, it enables us to thrive. It gives us the fuel to be active and creative, just as putting fuel in your car doesn't just prevent it from becoming derelict; it gives it the power to take you around. When it comes to the car there is no ambiguity about why we put fuel in: the fuel gauge tells us to. This is easy for us to grasp because man invented the car and there is no confusion about how it works.

Nature also provided us with a fuel gauge that is so sophisticated it doesn't only tell us when to fill up, it physically compels us to do so. That fuel gauge is the real reason why we eat and it is called **HUNGER.**

Eating isn't just a function of existence; it is a pleasure that we can all enjoy. Nature ensures we fulfil that pleasure by making us hungry.

Do you know what true hunger feels like? I'm sure you'll say you do, but many people go through life without ever experiencing true hunger. We're lucky enough to live in a part of the world where food is so readily available and such a major part of our lives that we never have to worry about where our next meal or snack is coming from.

We regard hunger as an affliction of the famine-stricken unfortunates who we watch with pity on television and give thanks that we are not them. It is a word that we associate with disaster. But there is a difference between hunger and starvation. Hunger is an incredible asset, a natural faculty of the human body that not only ensures we keep ourselves fuelled up, but actually enhances the pleasure of eating.

Hunger is triggered by a fall in the level of nutrients in the body. It is not a painful feeling, nor even an uncomfortable one. It only becomes unpleasant when you know you cannot satisfy it. There are two reasons why this might be the case: 1. You have no access to food and are in genuine danger of starvation; 2. You are denying yourself in accordance with some diet.

When you know that you are going to satisfy your hunger with delicious, nutritious food then it's easy to relax and enjoy the feeling for several hours without it ever becoming uncomfortable.

Hunger is also directly related to taste: the more hungry you are, the better the food seems to taste. This is how Nature enabled us to adapt to second- and third-rate foods when our favourite foods were not available. If you find the sight of celebrities eating witchetty grubs in the Australian jungle repulsive, try going several days in the outback without food. You'll soon begin to regard witchetty grubs as a delicacy.

By the same token, if you eat when you are not hungry, the food will taste bland and unsatisfying. If you are only eating because you've been conditioned to expect a certain taste, you will keep eating in the hope of getting that taste, just like a gambler pumping coins into a one-armed bandit in the hope of a payout that never comes.

The more you eat, the less satisfaction you get from the food you're eating. And if that food has nothing to offer in the way of nutritional satisfaction in the first place, then you are constantly chasing a hopeless cause.

WHAT'S ON THE MENU?

The human body is an incredible machine, both sophisticated and resilient, with the capacity to adapt and heal. But despite all the abuse we subject it too, its basic functions continue to work as they were designed to do. No matter how much rubbish we consume, hunger still works in the same way, trying to get us to eat the foods that we are designed to eat.

Hunger is the signal that your nutrient levels are running low and it is only switched off when you restore your nutrients to a satisfactory level. If the food you eat does not contain those vital nutrients, your hunger will not be satisfied. That's why you can go on eating crisps for hours without feeling full up. As far as your nutrient tank goes, you're still empty!

By the way, if you think crisps aren't part of your sugar problem because they're salty rather than sweet, think again. They are packed with sugar in the starch of the potatoes and you'll find added sugar in the flavourings too.

Let's clear away any more such confusion by going back to the foods we were designed to eat. Long before our ancestors learned how to preserve food, Nature's Guide enabled them to get the nutrients they needed by providing foods that were edible and tasted good in their natural state, i.e. without any need for cooking or other interventions.

These foods still taste good to us today. They are:

• Fruit

• Vegetables

• Nuts and seeds

These foods contain all the nutrients we need to survive. They are the foods we find easiest to digest and they leave very little waste once the nutrients have been extracted, so they neither use up much energy in the digestion process, nor leave behind deposits of excess fat. What's more, they will satisfy your hunger quickly and thoroughly so you won't feel compelled to overeat.

Fruit, vegetables and nuts and seeds are the foods Nature's Guide has designed for us to eat. They are the pinnacle of our favourite foods, but they are not the only things on the menu. Further down are the secondary foods to which Nature has enabled us to adapt. These foods will also give us the nutrients we require but they will do so less efficiently. Meat, for example, will give us protein, but it takes a lot more digesting and leaves a lot more waste. The energy required to process meat leaves us feeling sluggish. That's why cats and other carnivores spend so much time asleep.

So where does BAD SUGAR fit in to this menu? Quite simply, it doesn't fit in at all. Empty carbs give us none of the nutrients we need and so they never satisfy our hunger. The fuel gauge continues to signal empty so we never know when to stop eating. To compound the problem, the spike and crash effect on your blood sugar level creates an empty feeling that resembles hunger, a false hunger, which makes you eat when you don't need to.

We will look more closely at hunger in a later chapter. For now, follow the next instruction.

SEVENTH INSTRUCTION: AVOID EATING WHEN YOU'RE NOT HUNGRY

As long as you eat a diet consisting of BAD SUGAR, the balance between intake and output will always be out and you will never achieve the level of health and the kind of physique that you yearn for. It's easy to see the solution: cut out the BAD SUGAR. Now we need to show you how easy that can be in practice.

SUMMARY

- Disregard any preconceived target weight.
- We put on weight because our intake is greater than our output.
- Exercising to lose weight is like driving to burn off fuel.
- Diets are not the way to reduce intake.
- The more efficiently we satisfy hunger, the less we need to consume.
- Get the intake right and weight and disposal will take care of themselves.
- Refined sugar, processed and starchy carbs have no place on our menu.
- Avoid eating when you're not hungry.

Chapter 9

FEAR

All addicts are pulled apart by fears, all of them entirely illusory.

When you look at the facts about BAD SUGAR and its effect on the human body, when you take into account the massive rise in obesity and diabetes over the time that refined sugar and processed and starchy carbs have become such a ubiquitous part of our diet and when you consider that it neither tastes of much, nor gives us anything in the way of nutrition, you would think it would be easy to cut it out of your diet and think nothing more about it.

Well, guess what:

IT IS EASY!

The reason you, like millions of others, have not found it easy up until now is because you have been brainwashed into thinking that BAD SUGAR gives you some sort of pleasure or crutch.

Several years ago, there was an advertising campaign for cream cakes, which had the slogan "Naughty, but nice". It was a fiendishly clever piece of advertising, using an argument for NOT eating cream cakes to convince us to do the exact opposite. We all like the idea of being naughty. We associate naughtiness with fun, character, excitement. In the case of a cream cake, "naughty" means one thing and one thing alone:

THIS CAKE IS BAD FOR YOU

But aren't we so often drawn to things we know are bad for us because they seem to make life more interesting? People, pastimes, food and drink? This was exactly the mindset that the advertising campaign was exploiting. We all want to lead interesting lives. We fear drudgery. So we'll eat a cream cake, if it means we're being more exciting.

Would it have been more honest if the advertisers had used a stronger word than "naughty"? Certainly it would. Something that gives you diabetes is more than naughty, it's downright evil. Would it have put us off eating cream cakes, if they'd used the slogan "Evil but nice"? Probably not, because the same brainwashed thinking would still have applied. Smokers read the message "Smoking Kills" on every packet of cigarettes, but it doesn't stop them. If anything, it reinforces their belief that the cigarette must be giving them pleasure or a crutch. "If I know it's killing me, but I still want it so much, there must be something good about it."

Despite our knowledge of the disastrous effect BAD SUGAR can have on our health, we still make excuses for consuming it. Why? Because just as we fear the harmful effect it has on us, we also fear life without it.

We've explained about the tug-of-war that all addicts live with and the contradictory statements they come out with. "It makes me so miserable, but it's my one pleasure in life." On the one side of the tug-of-war is the fear of all the damage that BAD SUGAR is doing to our health; on the other side is fear caused by all the brainwashing: how could I cope without it? I'll be miserable! I'll never stay free!

Fear is a response that comes from both our instinct and our intellect. It is the instinct that drives us to fight or flight, alerting us to danger and making us wary in potentially dangerous situations. As such it is vital to our survival. But the things that make us afraid can be both real and imaginary. Our intellect has enabled us to learn about potential dangers and how to avoid them, so much so that we can be fearful of dangers of which there is no present evidence.

For example, the fears associated with losing your job are intellectual. You have learned about the possible consequences of finding yourself unemployed – e.g. having no money, being forced to sell your possessions, sacrificing the pleasures and comforts that you enjoy now, and so you do everything in your power to safeguard your job and make yourself indispensable, even when there is no threat of losing your job.

In this instance your intellect does you a good service. But what if your projected fears are based on false information? Say you read in a magazine that fruit causes cancer. You would probably avoid eating fruit. You would also worry about the damage already done by all the fruit you've eaten in your life.

No one, to my knowledge, has yet claimed that fruit causes cancer, but it is typical of the sort of scare stories with which we are bombarded on a regular basis. Some of them are based on sound evidence; others are nonsense. As consumers, it's impossible for us to know what to believe and we end up spending precious time worrying about things that will never happen – and, in the same confusion, being blasé about things that will.

FEAR IS THE BASIS OF ALL ADDICTION

It is the force that makes it seem difficult to quit when all logic tells us it should be easy. Fear is the ingenious con trick that keeps us in the trap. It is ingenious because it works back to front. It's when you are not consuming BAD SUGAR that you suffer the empty, insecure feeling. When you consume it, you feel a small boost, which partially relieves the insecurity and your brain is fooled into believing that the sugary food is providing a pleasure or crutch. In fact, it is BAD SUGAR that created the fear. The more you consume, the more it drags you down and the more apparent your need for the crutch.

This is why you, like all addicts, can never win while you're in the trap. When you're consuming BAD SUGAR, you wish you didn't have to. It's only when you can't have it that it appears to be precious. You mope for something that doesn't exist, an illusion: the perception of a pleasure or crutch.

FEAR OF FAILURE

Being addicted to BAD SUGAR is like being in a prison. Every aspect of your life is controlled by sugar: your daily routine, your hopes, your view of the world, your suffering. Of course, you're not physically imprisoned; there are no walls or bars. The prison is in your mind. However, as long as you remain a slave to BAD SUGAR, you will experience the same psychological symptoms as a convict in a physical prison.

If you've tried and failed to come off BAD SUGAR – or any other addiction – you will know that it leaves you feeling more firmly trapped than you did before. It's like a scene from a film in which a prisoner is thrown into a cell and the first thing he does is run to the door and wrench at the handle. This confirms his predicament: he really is locked in.

Trying and failing to conquer an addiction has the same effect on the addict. It reinforces the belief that you are trapped in a prison from which there is no escape. This can be a crushing experience and many people conclude that the best way to avoid the misery of failure is to avoid trying in the first place. The twisted thinking of the addict concludes that as long as you never try to escape, you will always preserve the belief that escape is possible. It is only when you try to escape that it becomes impossible.

You can clearly see how self-defeating this thinking is, yet there are millions of intelligent people around the world who continue to delude themselves in this way. They prefer to continue suffering the misery of addiction than risk the misery of failure. What they don't realize is that the person who tugs at the prison door and finds it firmly locked is using the wrong method of escape.

When channelled properly, the fear of failure can be a positive force. It's the response that focuses the mind of the runner on the starting blocks, the actress waiting in the wings and the student going into an exam. Fear of failure is the little voice in your head that reminds you to prepare thoroughly, to remember everything you've rehearsed and trained for, and to leave nothing to chance.

In the case of addiction, the fear of failure is illogical. It is the fear of something that has already happened. You are already a slave. You suffer a compulsion to keep stuffing yourself with BAD SUGAR, even though it's ruining your life and making you miserable. As long as that continues, you will always feel a failure.

The addict's fear of failure is based on the illusion that trying and failing will make you even more miserable than you are now. In reality, you have nothing to lose, even if you do fail. By not trying, you ensure that you remain permanently in the trap. In other words:

IF YOU SUCCUMB TO THE FEAR OF FAILURE, YOU ARE GUARANTEED TO SUFFER THE VERY THING YOU FEAR

But failure isn't the only fear that keeps addicts imprisoned in the trap.

FEAR OF SUCCESS

There is a syndrome among long-term convicts that drives many of them to reoffend soon after they are released from prison.

It's a depressing phenomenon, which occurs not because they are compulsive criminals who haven't learned the error of their ways, but because they actually *want* to go back inside. Life on the outside is alien and frightening for them; prison offers them a sense of security. It's the devil they know.

The same fear afflicts addicts. They regard life without their "crutch" as a prisoner regards life on the outside: they're afraid that they won't be able to enjoy or cope with life, that they'll have to go through some terrible trauma to get free and that they'll be condemned to a life of sacrifice and deprivation.

Perhaps you've been tricked into believing that life without BAD SUGAR is boring. You're well aware of the misery that your sugar addiction causes you, but you may have come to regard it as part of your identity.

The hopeless chocaholic who just can't help herself. Perhaps you think it gives you personality or makes you loveable. If your friends love you for your BAD SUGAR addiction, it's for one reason and one reason only:

IT MAKES THEM FEEL BETTER ABOUT THEIRS

All addicts love another addict; that's why they tend to group together. It's not because they find one another more interesting; it's because they find each other less threatening. You don't feel quite so stupid about your addiction when you're in the company of another addict.

Is that how you want to be loved? As the fool who makes

everyone else feel better by comparison? Or would you rather be loved and admired for your health and happy disposition?

HOW TO WIN THE TUG-OF-WAR

Remember what you've learned about the way addiction works: the panic feeling that makes you afraid to even try to cut BAD SUGAR out of your diet is caused by BAD SUGAR, not relieved by it. Once you quit, you will never suffer it again. The tug-of-war of fear may appear to you like a permanent struggle, but actually it is easy to win, because the fears pulling you from both sides are caused by the same thing: BAD SUGAR.

TAKE AWAY THE BAD SUGAR
AND THE FEAR GOES TOO

This method does not rely on tricks or gimmicks. It works through simple logic, replacing myths and illusions with the truth. But if there was one thing that would help the process, it would be a time machine. Then we could transport you into the future to the time when you finish reading this book and know just how good it feels to be free. Fear will have been replaced by elation, despair by optimism, self-doubt by confidence, apathy by dynamism. As a result of these psychological turnarounds, your physical health will improve too. You will enjoy a newfound energy, as well as the ability to truly relax.

Some people try to come off BAD SUGAR using other methods and manage to go for weeks or months without it, but still report that they miss it. This method is different. There is no sacrifice involved. You are not about to give up anything. You will not miss BAD SUGAR food. All you are doing is removing something from your life that has made you miserable and replacing it with something that makes you genuinely happy.

So get it clear in your mind:

THERE IS NOTHING TO FEAR

You are exchanging a lack of control over what you eat for total control – no choice for freedom of choice.

Part of you feels that BAD SUGAR is your friend, your companion and support, something you can always fall back on when you need a pick-me-up. This is an illusion. This sort of food is not food at all; it's your worst enemy. Far from supporting you, it's driving you deeper and deeper into misery. You instinctively know this, so open your mind and follow your instincts.

DITCH THE DOUBTS

Think about everything you stand to gain by getting rid of BAD SUGAR. Try to imagine the self-respect you'll feel, the time and energy you'll save not having to make excuses and pretend that you're in control. That little short-term illusory boost you feel every time you eat a cake or biscuit or chocolate bar or pizza or bowlful of pasta is how you'll feel all the time when you're free. The irony with all addictions is that the addict is constantly trying to feel like a non-addict feels all the time. The only way to do that is to quit being an addict.

In fact, how long do those illusory boosts even last? Not even as long as it takes to eat the junk. Before you've even finished eating it you start to feel guilty, remorseful, bloated, ashamed and out of shape. Imagine being free from those awful feelings forever. Imagine finishing every meal feeling FABULOUS, fit, healthy and happy.

If you had to witness a heroin addict suffering the misery of drug addiction, would you advise them to keep injecting heroin into their veins, rather than try living without that "high" they feel every time they get a fix? Of course you wouldn't. You would see that the "high" is nothing more than relief from the terrible craving that is caused by the drug as it leaves the body. It would be obvious to you that the only way to stop that craving would be to stop taking the drug.

Perhaps you don't think your problem is as severe as that of a heroin addict. That's because, in spite of Hollywood's attempts to brainwash us to the contrary, pretty much everything you've ever heard about heroin is negative, whereas you've been brainwashed into believing that BAD SUGAR can be a positive. The truth is that both do absolutely nothing for you whatsoever, both destroy your health, destroy your self-esteem, enslave you and make you miserable.

All addicts are caught in the same trap. See yourself as you would see a heroin addict and give yourself the only logical piece of advice:

CUT OUT THE BAD SUGAR NOW!

It's as simple as that. The only reason you might fail to see the solution as simple is because you've been brainwashed into the tug-of-war of fear. Once you can see that there is nothing to fear, that you are not giving up anything or depriving yourself in any way, quitting is easy.

In his own words – Jack, a "BAD SUGAR" addict who got free using Allen Carr's Easyway:

All my life I've been overweight. From my very first memory it seemed that I was out of shape. I loved playing soccer, but often couldn't keep up with play because of the extra weight I was carrying.

When I look back at photos of myself in childhood, I actually wasn't hugely overweight, just enough to stand out as being a bit chubby. The same applied all the way through adolescence and young adulthood. Definitely overweight, but not terribly so.

My favourite foods were always pizza, sandwiches, pasta and potatoes of every description (fried, roasted or mashed, not forgetting crisps). I never used to eat a lot of sweet stuff, but my diet was made up almost entirely of processed or starchy carbohydrate. Don't get me wrong – I could eat my way through a whole pack of biscuits and as many chocolate bars or as much ice cream as might be put in front of me and there were certainly times when I would binge on that kind of food.

As I reached my thirties and moved into my forties, it became apparent that I was gaining more and more weight, to the point where I was deeply embarrassed and ashamed of how I looked. It was strange how quickly I moved on from the moment of realization, the feeling of self-loathing and self-disgust, to just accepting that this was just the way I was. I tried my best never to be photographed. Ever! I felt embarrassed for my kids because I could imagine what their school friends might think of them having such an overweight father. I look at photographs that were taken of me in my forties; there are only a few, and it makes me want to weep for the man pictured. I feel a strange kind of detachment from him. I feel immense sympathy for him, regret for him, but overwhelmingly I feel incalculable relief that I escaped from being him.

How did I do it? I realized that I was addicted to BAD SUGAR. Within 14 months of avoiding it, I had lost more than 70 pounds. To my astonishment, and to the astonishment of my wife, my kids, my family and my friends, it wasn't even difficult. In fact it was ridiculously easy and enjoyable.

I couldn't ever imagine living without eating fries or pasta or potatoes or rice or noodles or bread, but within days of cutting them out of my diet, I simply didn't want them anymore. I think my brain understood that they were poison to me and from that moment my instinct took over.

I recall as if it were yesterday, the day that my life changed forever. I'd had a routine health check with my doctor and she delivered the bad news to me: "Sorry, you have Type 2 diabetes and need to start medication immediately." It was like a punch in the face. She talked about the future prospect and danger of potential organ failure, amputation, eyesight failure. Stuff that, I'm ashamed to admit, I'd never known could be affected by weight gain ultimately leading to Type 2 diabetes. I hadn't even known that being so overweight made me almost certain to become a Type 2 diabetic.

I was given a handful of leaflets describing what my diet should be and what kind of medication I would need to take. I walked out of the doctor's office reeling from the news.

But very quickly something stirred in me. I remembered a newspaper article I'd read the previous year that described how a Type 2 diabetes sufferer had moved to the USA through his job and when he went to his first consultation with his US doctor and described the eating programme he followed under the advice of his English doctor, his US physician described it as "suicidal". I have no idea why I remembered the newspaper story, I think it resonated with me because it talked about how the guy with diabetes was eating processed and starchy carbohydrate with every meal and it was this that the US doctor found so unbelievable. I think it stood out for me because deep down I suspected that my problems with weight were caused by an addiction to what I understand now to be BAD SUGAR.

My doctor had told me that my HbA1c fasting blood test results were extremely high. She'd even done a retest to double-check. The HbA1c test indicates your blood glucose levels for the previous two to three months. It does this by measuring the amount of glucose that is being carried by the red blood cells in the body. The result was categoric. I was Type 2 diabetic and faced a lifetime of medication and ongoing tests to protect my health.

Somewhere, it just didn't sit right with me. I don't know why or how, but I knew deep inside that it just wasn't right.

From that moment onwards, I eradicated some simple foods from my diet. No potato in any form. No rice. No bread (other than a thin slice of wholemeal toast in the morning with my breakfast). No pasta. No refined sugar (such as desserts, sweets or pastries). No fruit juice.

I'd stopped smoking with Allen Carr's Easyway and

it was so easy to apply the same mindset to this issue.

I focused on eating plenty of fresh, healthy food, fruit, vegetables, salads – always making sure that if I ate meat it was in reasonably small portions with plenty of salad. I didn't eliminate dairy entirely, I just made sure that I didn't have milk and only had a little cheese every now and then (aside from a small amount of feta crumbled into my salad).

I was never hungry and enjoyed what I was eating. For the first month or two, I even avoided alcohol. I just wanted to see if I could get better.

Just TWO DAYS after I started my new way of eating, I purchased a blood glucose monitor, a simple device to test blood sugar levels. The first reading I got was in the normal range. Normal! The second reading I got was normal. Over the coming days, every reading I took was absolutely normal. I was thrilled. I was hopeful. More importantly, I felt amazing. Within a couple of weeks the weight began to fall off me. Only a pound or two most weeks, but it was steady and it was easy.

I made an appointment to see my doctor again. I explained that I had taken my own blood sugar readings and that they indicated I was normal. She was dismissive and almost aggressive and was determined that I begin taking diabetic medication. She dismissed my daily blood sugar readings saying that the test that really mattered was the HbA1c and that given that test covers two to three months she'd test me again in just under three months' time. I carried on testing myself and continued to get only normal results. Even when I began to allow myself a beer or two on a Friday night, the results remained well within the normal range.

By the time I went back for the next HbA1c test, I'd already lost 20 pounds and lost three inches off my waist. I'd had to buy new trousers and jeans.

The doctor was surprised by the results of the HbA1c test. They were normal. Yet she still encouraged me to start taking medication and made an appointment for me to see a nutritionist. By the time I had the appointment with the nutritionist, I had lost more than 40 pounds and had moved up another three holes on my belt (my waist having reduced by more than five inches) and was feeling fabulous and still having normal blood readings every single time I checked. The nutritionist bizarrely described the way I was eating as "inadvisable" and suggested that I start each day with a glass of orange juice (the effect of which is like a sugar bomb) and that I should eat starchy carbs (a third of a plate) with every meal. I couldn't believe it; the nutritionist, who was young enough to be newly qualified, actually recommended that I eat the very foods that had nearly killed me! I told her about my weight loss and showed her the old holes on my belt, explaining that I was making regular trips to the local cobbler to have him punch extra holes in my belt. She was unmoved and maintained that her advice was good. I ignored it, thank goodness, and continued to lose weight and inches around my waist. I saw amazing changes; even my feet looked in better shape – basically, less chubby. A year later, I returned for another check-up, 70 pounds lighter and more than nine inches slimmer around the waist. By now I was on first name terms with my cobbler. I'd only get one extra hole punched in my belt at a time – it was so enjoyable knowing that before too long I'd be back for another.

More than four years has passed since my diagnosis. Never once have I had a bad blood sugar reading either with the device I use at home, or with the HbA1c test.

Fairly soon after I had started eating better, I became more inclined to exercise. I started taking the train to work rather than driving. The 15-minute walk to the station was fabulous, and not sitting in traffic every morning and evening was amazing for my stress levels. The commute made sure that I at least moved my body a little. I had been shocked when I thought about my sedentary lifestyle, I'd only been walking a few yards to my car on my drive and a few yards from my work parking space to my desk, that was it! I was never really into going to the gym and didn't feel that I wanted to dedicate time to that kind of thing, but being a rail user meant that instead of sitting in my car for 45 minutes each morning and evening, I was getting a 15-minute walk. I started listening to music, audio books, and radio podcasts while I walked and after a few months realized that if I walked 30 minutes to a railway station on a different line, it would only add five minutes to my commute and boost my walking by 100 per cent. I went for it and enjoyed every single step, every single day, through spring, summer, autumn and winter. The fact is it was changing my eating that created the weight loss. The exercise was a wonderful bonus and incredibly healthy change in lifestyle.

Over the past few years, I've noticed that the mainstream medical profession has started looking into low-carb diets to handle Type 2 diabetes, but there still seems to be an automatic assumption that upon diagnosis someone with the disease needs to be medicated (and keep on having a third of a plate of starchy carbs with every meal). I was amazed to find out that several diabetes charities were funded in a significant way by pharmaceutical companies that manufacture the medication for the disease and food companies that produce and sell BAD SUGAR foods. Even today, the diabetes charities in the UK remain "sniffy" about sufferers freeing themselves from the disease by changing their diet. The fact that they refer to "recommended intake of carbohydrates", rather than differentiating between good sugar and BAD SUGAR, indicates a complete lack of competence (at best) or outside influences (at worst).

I do owe my life to my doctor – if she hadn't tested me for Type 2 who knows whether I would ever have become free. I also owe my life to the writer of the article I read the year before my diagnosis. I've spent hours trying to track the article down on the internet, but never succeeded. Aside from that, and most of all, I owe my life to Allen Carr's Easyway. Stopping smoking easily changed my life forever, and applying the same principles to BAD SUGAR made the whole process of losing weight and becoming healthier not just easy, but incredibly enjoyable, effortless and, more importantly, long-lasting.

FEAR OF THE PROCESS

There is one further fear that might be preventing you from winning the tug-of-war. You may be afraid that the process itself will be painful. If you've struggled to cut out sugar before by using willpower, you may remember it as a torturous experience. That's because the willpower method doesn't work. As I will explain in the next chapter, it actually makes quitting harder.

So forget your past attempts to quit. See that your failures were down to using the wrong method. The fact that you've found it impossible to quit up until now has no bearing on the fact that you want to quit. That has never gone away.

EIGHTH INSTRUCTION: NEVER DOUBT YOUR DECISION TO QUIT

Your desire to conquer your sugar addiction is the reason you're reading this book. Keep that in mind as you read on, think about everything we've established so far and be clear that you understand and accept it. If you are struggling with any of the instructions, go back and re-read the relevant chapter until it becomes clear. It is essential that you not only follow the instructions, but also that you understand and accept them.

If you follow all the instructions, you will no longer feel the desire for BAD SUGAR. The desire to quit will win out and the prison door will spring open.

```
┌───────────── SUMMARY ─────────────┐
│                                             │
│ • Addicts are constantly pulled in two directions by the tug-of- │
│   war of fear.                              │
│                                             │
│ • Succumb to the fear of failure and you guarantee failure. │
│                                             │
│ • The fear of success is based on illusions. │
│                                             │
│ • Cut out BAD SUGAR and all the fears go too. │
│                                             │
│ • Open your mind to everything you stand to gain. │
│                                             │
│ • There is no physical or mental trauma in quitting. │
│                                             │
│ • Never doubt your decision to quit. There is nothing to fear. │
│                                             │
└─────────────────────────────────┘
```

SUGAR MYTHS – THE BIG SEVEN
(These are the myths we tell ourselves about sugar)

"It's a social thing."

Are you saying if you're home alone and there's fudge cake in the fridge, it goes untouched? The fact is that, when you binge with someone else, it feels like you at least have a partner in crime. It makes you feel less awful about yourself. Yet somewhere along the line the guilt and the self-disgust still haunt you.

"It gives me a burst of energy and it's my way of relaxing and chilling out."

Can you see the ridiculous contradiction in those two claims? As a sugar addict you're incapable of relaxing without feeding that Little Monster. That's not the same as sugar helping you to relax. It's like wearing tight shoes just for the relief of taking them off.

One of the saddest things about the modern-day sugar trap – and for that matter the caffeine trap – is that perfectly healthy, vivacious, athletic, and energetic kids are being conned into believing they have to drink caffeine-loaded "sugar bombs" to take part in sports or simple leisure pursuits. As they get older, they're even conned into drinking the same kind of caffeine and sugar bombs with their first experiences of drinking alcohol.

Even as an adult, your natural state should be to feel energized anyway. If you're not sick, you should have more than enough energy to enjoy whatever you want to do in life. If you really are tired, then your body is asking for sleep and rest, not BAD SUGAR.

Using BAD SUGAR for energy is like taking out a payday loan.

A quick injection of cash (energy) and they've got you hooked in, with interest, for the rest of your life, with you having to go back for more again and again and again until you do something about it. The reality is that sugar addiction makes you permanently tired and exhausted. Take a look at anyone with a sugar problem. They invariably look tired, run-down and ready to drop. The irony is that the only thing that's stopping them returning to their energetic, athletic, vivacious former self is the one thing they think they need to function – BAD SUGAR.

For the few occasions in life when we need a little help to get through a late shift or to keep us going until the end of a long day there are many natural, harmless, non-addictive, and healthy stimulants to help temporarily carry us through. The fact is, if you get BAD SUGAR out of your life, you won't feel in need of them anyway. You'll be brimming with energy.

"I love the smell."
That's fine but I love the smell of any number of perfumes and aftershaves yet I have no desire or need to drink them!

"It's my comfort food."
This is the biggest fraud of all. When a BAD SUGAR addict is happy, what do they do? They eat sugar. When a BAD SUGAR addict is sad what do they do? They eat sugar. As an addict they're incapable of doing anything without a constant supply of the drug to which they are addicted. And the biggest fraud about "comfort" eating? It makes you feel lousy about yourself: guilty,

ashamed and disgusted. There's nothing comforting about it. All you're doing is feeding the Little Monster.

"It's my treat or reward."
You don't choose to consume BAD SUGAR. If you had any choice whether to do so or not, you wouldn't be reading this book. As a BAD SUGAR addict you're incapable of doing anything without having BAD SUGAR before, during and after. It's not a reward or treat system; it's simply drug addiction.

"I love the taste."
Yet you'd eat an entire box of chocolates, even the ones you don't really like. Be honest: there are times you wolf the stuff down so quickly you can't even pretend to be savouring the taste. Does that sound like it has anything to do with liking the taste, or does that just sound like you're feeding the Little Monster? If it was anything to do with taste, why do you swallow it? Why not just spit it out?

Why haven't Mars made sugar-free M&Ms? For the same reason tobacco companies don't sell nicotine-free cigarettes: neither of these addictions are about taste; they're just about getting your fix.

"Chocolate is better than sex!"
If you really believe that, you don't just need to quit sugar, you need to find a new partner… and fast!

Chapter 10

WILLPOWER

IN THIS CHAPTER
• *TAKING THE DIFFICULT OPTION*
• *WHO ARE YOU CALLING WEAK-WILLED?*
• *A NEVER-ENDING STRUGGLE* • *CROSSING THE LINE THE EASY WAY*
• *BRAGGERS AND WHINGERS*

Addiction makes us feel helpless. We assume that our inability to quit is due to a weakness in our character. More often than not, the opposite is true.

How many times have you said, "Oh, I just can't resist," or something of that nature, when presented with a cake, chocolates or biscuits? Just at that moment when you told yourself you'd be strong and not give in to temptation, your resolve deserts you and you find yourself reaching for the sugar. If only you had more willpower.

The assumption that quitting any addiction requires willpower comes from the widespread belief that the process is hard. This belief is put about not only by the industries that peddle their poison, but also by the medical professionals who spend their time trying to remedy it. Would you say, "I just can't resist," if it was widely accepted that resistance is easy? Of course not.

The only reason people find it hard to quit is because they use the wrong method. And they use the wrong method because they believe it's hard to quit.

Say you were in a prison cell and someone told you you could open the door by pushing in a certain place, but added that it was an extremely heavy door and it would take all your strength to open it.

You push where they tell you to and find that it is indeed very hard. You really put your back into it and push as hard as you can. The door budges a little, but eventually your strength gives out and the door slams shut again.

You conclude two things:

1. You failed to escape because you are not strong enough.

2. You will never be able to escape.

This is exactly what happens when you try to quit using the willpower method.

Now imagine you're sitting there in that cell, desperate to escape, but thinking you lack the strength to do so.

Another visitor comes along and tells you you've been pushing on the wrong part of the door, where the hinges are. They tell you that if you push on the other side the door will open easily. Would you give it a try, or would you continue to believe the only way to escape is the impossible way?

That's the difference between Easyway and the willpower

method: one works, the other doesn't; one is easy, the other is so hard as to be impossible.

THE WILLPOWER METHOD ALWAYS FAILS

People who try to quit with the willpower method endure a constant conflict of will, a mental tug-of-war. On one side your rational brain knows you should stop eating sugar because it's making you unhealthy, affecting your happiness and self-esteem. On the other side, your addicted brain makes you panic at the thought of being deprived of your pleasure or crutch.

With the willpower method you try to focus on all the reasons for stopping and hope you can stay strong for long enough without BAD SUGAR for the desire to eventually go. The problem with this is that you still see BAD SUGAR as a pleasure or a crutch and so you feel that you've made a sacrifice.

At the beginning, you might feel good about this sacrifice. After all, everything has its price, right? And if you want it badly enough the price is always worth paying.

But how long can you keep paying for? The trouble with sacrifice is that eventually you begin to resent it. You effectively force yourself into a self-imposed tantrum, like a child being deprived of its toys.

It's not a wholesome, cleansing feeling any more, it's a miserable feeling, which makes you want to try to cheer yourself up. And how do you do that? With the one thing you've vowed not to do – YOU EAT BAD SUGAR.

Now you feel doubly miserable. You see yourself as a

failure because you have not been able to resist the temptation and, at the same time, the sugar hasn't made you happy, it's only made you want more sugar again and your belief that you can't live without it has been reinforced. As a result of trying to quit with the willpower method, you're more addicted than you were before.

YOU ONLY NEED WILLPOWER IF YOU HAVE A CONFLICT OF WILL

Addicts want to quit because they're afraid of the consequences, but they are scared to quit because they are afraid of life without their little crutch. One fear is rational, the other is irrational, yet when you're in the trap they are both very real.

We have already begun to unravel the illusion that you will be making a sacrifice by cutting BAD SUGAR out of your diet. We will continue to unravel it, not by focusing on all the negatives you will suffer if you don't stop but by recognizing all the positives you will enjoy when you do. As you come to see that there is absolutely nothing to fear and so much to look forward to in a life without sugar, you will remove the conflict and find it easy to win the tug-of-war.

EXCEPTIONS

As with every rule, there are always exceptions. Some people do manage to quit smoking, drinking, overeating and other addictions through sheer force of will, but they never actually break free of their addiction, so they never achieve the true, relaxed state of happiness that you will achieve. They live the rest of their lives believing they have made a sacrifice.

HOW WEAK-WILLED ARE YOU?

So you assume that you are weak-willed because you have failed to control your eating in the past. That is generally how society regards people with an eating problem; they lack the willpower to control themselves. Indeed, that is generally how people with eating problems regard themselves. They assume it's they who have failed, not the method. No one questions the willpower method except Easyway.

If you still think that it's a lack of willpower that has kept you hooked on BAD SUGAR, then you haven't yet understood the nature of the trap you're in. Remember, the trap works in reverse: it makes the addict desire the very thing that's tormenting him.

Maybe there are other ways in which you think you're weak-willed. Perhaps you're a smoker, or you gamble, or drink too much and you regard these conditions as further evidence of a weak will. There is a connection between all addictions, but the connection is not that they are signs of a lack of willpower. On the contrary, they are more likely evidence of a strong will. What they all share is that they are traps created by misleading information and untruths. And one of the most misleading untruths is that quitting requires willpower.

IT TAKES A STRONG WILL TO PERSIST IN DOING
SOMETHING THAT GOES AGAINST
ALL YOUR INSTINCTS

When you organize your life so you can sneak to the shops to buy sweets or cakes without arousing suspicion; when you get up early in the morning or stay up late at night so you can eat without anyone looking over your shoulder; when you give up the pastimes you used to enjoy... all these actions take a strong will.

Anyone who saw you trying to open a door by pushing on the hinges, despite being told you'd find it easier if you pushed on the handle, would call you wilful, not weak-willed.

Think of people you know who have eating problems. Are they all weak-willed types? Think of all the famous people who are overweight; did they reach their high-profile position by giving up easily? Prime ministers, film directors, captains of industry, movie stars, singers, even some sports stars – the evidence of eating problems is clear to see. Yet the common ground between them all is that they reached their positions through sheer determination and nothing less.

In other words, they had immense willpower. So why would their willpower fail them in this one area?

Now think how you react when people tell you that you have to change your ways and sort out your diet? Doesn't it make you want to do the opposite? Wouldn't you describe that as wilful? In fact, it tends to be the most strong-willed people who find it hardest to quit by using the willpower method, because when the door fails to open, they won't give up and look for an easier method, they'll force themselves to keep pushing on the hinges until they can push no more. Most of the people who are reading this book will have failed to control their eating again, and again, and again. Yet here they are, reading this book, they never gave up. That's grit, determination and terrific willpower. Don't sell yourself short. It's not lack of willpower that has trapped you: it's simply BAD SUGAR addiction.

Imagine running a marathon in tight shoes. It's painful, but you're determined to complete the course, so you struggle on. The further you go, the more it hurts, but at the same time you know you're getting closer to the finish, so the fear of failure increases. When you try to quit by the willpower method, the struggle never ends. As long as you believe that you're giving something up, you will always be running in pain. The stronger your will, the longer you will withstand the agony and the more powerful your craving will be. When you finally give in, you will be convinced you must have been within touching distance of success and you will despise yourself all the more for falling so close to the line. But what you don't realize is that

WITH THE WILLPOWER METHOD, THERE IS NO FINISH LINE

CROSSING THE LINE THE EASY WAY

With Easyway, you cross the finish line as soon as you remove the fear and illusions and stop consuming BAD SUGAR. That's when you are free of the addiction. It's that easy. Conversely, you will not get to that line if you use willpower and force yourself to suffer.

Addicts will go to great lengths to get their fix, be it nicotine, gambling, junk-spending, heroin, BAD SUGAR, whatever. Try stopping them and see how strong-willed they are. The hard-line approach will not work; it will only make them more entrenched in their addiction because:

1. It makes them feel foolish and scared of what they're doing to themselves. The fear the addict feels reinforces the myth that quitting is hard.

2. It creates a panic feeling: How will I cope? What will life be like when I quit? How will I survive? Which in turn creates a feeling of fear and deprivation, which the addict will seek to alleviate in their usual way: they will fall back into the trap.

It's fear that keeps them hooked. Fear of what will happen if they carry on versus fear of what will happen if they stop.

When you fail on the willpower method, it's even harder to try again because you will have reinforced the belief that it is impossible to cure your problem. If you've tried the willpower method and failed you may recall an enormous sense of relief when you gave in and had that first binge on chocolate or blowout meal. It's important to understand that this relief was nothing more than a temporary end to the self-inflicted pain. You didn't think, "Thank goodness for that! I've fallen back into the sugar trap." It is not a pleasure. In fact, it is accompanied by feelings of failure and foreboding, guilt and disappointment.

That first fix after you've tried to quit is not pleasurable at all, despite what others might tell you. They're confusing pleasure with the relief of ending a period of intense dissatisfaction. It's nothing more than the feeling of relief you get when you take off a pair of tight shoes. Would you wear tight shoes just for the relief of taking them off?

BRAGGERS AND WHINGERS

Other people who try to quit by the willpower method can have a harmful effect on your own desire to quit. They fall into two camps: "the braggers", who spend their time boasting about the sacrifices they're making; and "the whingers", who can't help moaning about the sacrifices they make. Both camps reinforce the misconception that quitting is hard and demands endless willpower and sacrifice.

NINTH INSTRUCTION: IGNORE THE ADVICE OF ANYONE WHO CLAIMS TO HAVE QUIT BY THE WILLPOWER METHOD

The beautiful truth is there is absolutely no sacrifice. You are not "giving up" anything. You only need willpower if you are caught up in a conflict of wills. Take away the fear of being deprived and there is nothing to tug against. It's easy.

People who quit with the willpower method are always waiting: waiting for the moment when they no longer feel deprived and, therefore, no longer need to apply their willpower. It's a moment that never comes for them. They can push the door open far enough to see the light and feel the fresh air of freedom but they never actually escape, regardless of what they might tell you. Let's face it, if you went to all that trouble, would you admit that you had failed?

There is nothing to wait for. Your happiness begins the moment you unravel all the illusions that have led you into the sugar trap, free yourself from fear and stop eating BAD SUGAR. It will happen with a feeling of excitement and elation.

I deliberately refer to BAD SUGAR throughout this book. I make no apology for doing so. Part of the brainwashing you've suffered all your life has been misdirection. When you think about sugar, you think of sweets, chocolate, cakes, pastries, puddings, desserts and donuts and the like. Did it ever occur to you that something as simple as bread was causing you a major problem? Perhaps. What about pasta, rice and potato? Did it ever occur to you that by continuing to eat those "foods" you were actually maintaining an addiction to BAD SUGAR that made it virtually impossible for you to abstain from the more obviously sugary foods that you traditionally considered your only enemy?

If you've followed all the instructions and understood that the beliefs that kept you in the sugar trap are fake, phony and illusory, that you are not required to summon any willpower to resist the temptation from BAD SUGAR because there is no temptation and that there is nothing to fear because life without BAD SUGAR will be unimaginably better than it is now, then you should already be feeling a sense of elation and anticipation. You have taken a major step in solving your eating problem. You can start living your life again, knowing that you are no longer a slave to sugar. You are in control and soon you will be free.

There is only one more obstacle that might be preventing you from feeling this sense of elation. Not everyone who tries and fails to stop by using the willpower method concludes that they are weak-willed, but rather than look for the true reasons why they remain hooked, they decide it must be down to another aspect of their personality over which they have no control. When all other explanations fail them, there is one theory that conveniently provides the excuse they need to stay in the trap: the so-called "addictive personality".

SUMMARY

- Quitting is only hard if you use the wrong method.
- Addiction is not a symptom of being weak-willed. It is often the opposite.
- With the willpower method, you never reach the finish line.
- People who brag or whinge about quitting by willpower still believe they are making a sacrifice.
- With Easyway, you cross the line the moment you reverse the brainwashing and cut out the sugar.

Chapter 11

THE ADDICTIVE PERSONALITY

IN THIS CHAPTER
•A CONVENIENT EXCUSE •WHY SOME PEOPLE SEEM TO BE MORE SUSCEPTIBLE THAN OTHERS •A DIFFERENT BREED •THE EVIDENCE OF HISTORY •THE EFFECT, NOT THE CAUSE •THE MONSTERS WITHIN •ACCEPTANCE

The theory of the addictive personality stems from looking at the situation from the wrong perspective. Any character traits shared by addicts are not the cause of their addiction; they are the result.

As someone who has experienced struggles with their eating, you'll know how the problem can leave you feeling confused and foolish. You can't understand why you can apply your will to other aspects of your life, but when it comes to eating you feel weak and helpless. Until you can see the nature of the trap you're in and understand that it has nothing to do with willpower, it is natural to assume that the problem lies with you. As a response, you make up excuses in an attempt to explain your illogical condition.

"You only live once – you've got to enjoy yourself a little."

"It's only food – it's not like I'm a heroin addict or anything."

"I can always cut it out – just not right now."

We can all see the absurdity in these excuses, but when you still believe that sugar gives you some sort of pleasure or crutch, you cling to anything that allows you to continue eating it despite all the good reasons for quitting. Even people who are told their problem is addiction are ready with an excuse:

"I have an addictive personality."

The addictive personality theory is a godsend for addicts who refuse to open their minds to the possibility that there is an easy cure. It gives them an excuse to avoid their fear of success by not even trying to quit.

And it allows them to pity themselves rather than despise themselves, as they continue to slide deeper and deeper into the trap. How tragic! To believe that you are born with a genetic predisposition to self-destruction.

The thinking goes like this: some people have a flaw in their genetic make-up that makes them more susceptible than most to becoming hooked. This thinking has been lent weight by so-called "experts", who have bandied the term "addictive personality" about so often that it's easy to be fooled into believing that it's an established condition.

It is not. It's a theory and nothing more, largely based on the incidence of multiple addictions in the same people and within families, e.g. drinkers who are also smokers or gamblers, or heroin addicts who smoke and are heavily in debt, or alcoholics whose parents were also alcoholics.

You probably know people who fit the description of the multiple addict. Perhaps you're one yourself. Smoking, drinking, gambling, overeating – they do seem to coincide in a lot of people, don't they?

In fact, all these addictions are caused by the same thing, but it's nothing to do with your personality or genetics. It's simply the misguided belief that the thing you are addicted to gives you a genuine pleasure or crutch.

CONFUSING THE BIG MONSTER FOR PERSONALITY

Despite the fact that millions of people suffer with the same problem, addiction is a lonely condition. Addicts become very insular and convince themselves that they are suffering with a problem that's unique to them.

The addictive personality or gene theory can be reinforced by failed attempts to quit by the willpower method. If you put all your effort into something but still fail, it's natural to assume that it's beyond your power to solve. Similarly, people who have quit by the willpower method (the braggers and whingers) also add weight to the theory. If they can abstain for years, yet still crave their little crutch, surely there must be some flaw in their make-up that keeps trying to pull them back?

But there is another explanation: they are still under the illusion that BAD SUGAR gives them pleasure or a crutch.

Earlier we introduced you to the Little Monster and the Big Monster. The Little Monster is the addiction; the mild, slightly empty, slightly restless feeling you get when BAD SUGAR is withdrawing from your body; the Big Monster is the belief that BAD SUGAR foods are enjoyable, pleasurable, rewarding and beneficial and that the feeling you get when you temporarily relieve the withdrawal by eating or drinking more BAD SUGAR is genuine relief or pleasure. The longer you fight the feeling of deprivation, the worse it seems to get, and the greater the relief and pleasure appears to be when you finally cave in. The willpower method focuses only on killing the Little Monster. We think if we can go long enough without the drug, eventually it will leave our body entirely and the desire for it will disappear. The willpower method ignores the Big Monster and, in fact, makes it stronger by encouraging the belief that you are making a sacrifice.

It's not just the Little Monster that can arouse the Big Monster; all sorts of things can trigger it: a trauma, a social occasion, a smell, a picture… as long as you allow the Big Monster to remain alive in your head, you will always be vulnerable to a feeling of deprivation and a craving for BAD SUGAR. Braggers and whingers kill off the Little Monster within days of quitting but they never kill the Big Monster.

THE SO-CALLED ADDICTIVE PERSONALITY IS NOTHING MORE THAN THE BIG MONSTER AT LARGE

Killing the Big Monster is easy, provided you keep an open mind. If you cling to the excuse that you have an addictive personality or gene, it means that your mind is not open and you risk sentencing yourself to a lifetime of slavery.

Even if there was such a thing as an addictive personality or gene and you had it, Easyway would still set you free because the addiction is actually easy to break as long as you get rid of the brainwashing: the Big Monster.

FILLING A VOID

So why do some people fall deeper into the trap than others? Why can one person have the occasional chocolate, while another eats the whole box in one go? Doesn't that suggest that one has a personality that's more prone to addiction than the other?

It does point to a difference between them, yes, but the difference lies in their conditioning, not in their genetic make-up. We are conditioned by all sorts of things: upbringing, peer pressure, education, income, opportunity. From the moment we are born we are prone to feelings of emptiness, a void, which is filled by our parents' love and affection. As we grow older and we see the flaws in our parents and the fairytales they've told us, the void opens up and we try to fill it with other things: heroes, friends, social status. We become susceptible to smoking, drinking, overeating and other addictions.

For some people the void is greater than for others because of their upbringing, the environment in which they live and a whole host of other factors.

Such factors will determine how much and how often we eat, as do the restrictions in our lives. Some people only eat a packet of biscuits a week because that's all they can afford. Some are allowed to eat at work; others are not. But if all restrictions were taken out of our way, we would all tend towards eating more BAD SUGAR, not less, because that's how addiction works.

The people who fall deepest into the trap have the greatest opportunity, the most money and the greatest desire because of the way they have been conditioned. You may regard them as hopeless cases. Easyway has seen countless such "hopeless cases" released from the trap simply by reversing the conditioning, unravelling the brainwashing and helping them to realize that their little crutch is actually their mortal enemy.

As well as noticing that some people fall deeper into the trap than others, no doubt you will also have noticed those people who don't fall into the trap at all – those lucky ones who can happily say no when the chocolates are wafted under their nose – seem to be a different breed.

You feel much more comfortable with your fellow addicts and you appear to share similar character traits: an unstable temperament, which swings between exuberance and misery, a tendency towards excess, a high susceptibility to stress, evasiveness, anxiety, insecurity. Doesn't this suggest there's a shared personality trait that has led to you having an eating problem?

Remember what you learned in Chapter 5: the difference between a BAD SUGAR addict and a non-sugar addict is that the latter has absolutely no desire for BAD SUGAR foods.

THE DESIRE TO EAT BAD SUGAR IS CAUSED BY EATING BAD SUGAR

The reason people with an eating problem feel more comfortable in the company of similar addicts is not because they're more laid-back or fun; on the contrary, the attraction lies in the fact that they won't challenge you or make you think twice about your addiction, because they're in the same boat. All addicts know they're doing something stupid and self-destructive. If you're surrounded by other people doing the same thing, you don't feel quite so foolish.

The good news is that, once you're free from BAD SUGAR addiction, you also get free from the harmful effect it has on your character, your personality, and your self-esteem as well as the obvious impact it has on your health. You just need to understand that you didn't become addicted to sugar because you have an addictive personality or gene.

The addiction fools you into believing that you're dependent on sugar and that there's some weakness in your character or genetic make-up. It distorts your perceptions and thus maintains its grip on you.

HISTORICAL EVIDENCE

If there was a gene that predisposed people to become addicts, you would expect the percentage of addicts in the world to have remained fairly constant throughout history. Yet this is not the case. Take smoking, for example. In the 1940s more than 80 per cent of the UK adult male population was hooked on nicotine; today it's fewer than 25 per cent. A similar trend is evident throughout most of Western Europe and North America. So are we to conclude that the proportion of people with addictive personalities has fallen by a whopping 55 per cent in just over half a century?

At the same time, the number of smokers in Asia has soared. What complex genetic anomaly is this that rises and falls so rapidly, and even appears to transfer itself wholesale from one continent to another?

KNOW YOUR ENEMY

It might feel to you that you have a battle to win, a battle against two monsters. But if you understand how the Little Monster and Big Monster work and how they've manipulated you all your life you will find it easy to conquer them.

The Little Monster was created the first time you were given BAD SUGAR. It would have been before you were even capable of conscious thought. Likewise, you were also a victim of the Big Monster in the same way – before you were even capable of conscious thought. You were brainwashed into believing that BAD SUGAR was a treat or reward by the most influential people on this planet who, ironically, loved you and cared for you most: your parents. No wonder you believed that BAD SUGAR was good! The Little Monster feeds on BAD SUGAR food and drink and when you don't give it what it wants, it begins to complain. This feeling is barely perceptible, like a slight itch, but it acts as a trigger. It arouses the Big Monster.

This Big Monster is not physical, but psychological. It is created by all the brainwashing that has led you to believe that BAD SUGAR gives you pleasure or provides some kind of benefit or crutch. It interprets the Little Monster's complaints as "I need sugar". Trying to please the Big Monster means trying to satisfy a craving by doing the very thing that caused the craving in the first place.

Every time you consume BAD SUGAR, it temporarily quietens the Little Monster, creating the illusion that the BAD SUGAR has made you relaxed and happy.

In fact, all it has done is taken you from feeling miserable and restless to feeling "OK". "OK" is how someone who is not manipulated by BAD SUGAR feels all the time. It is a natural state of contentment. But as someone who is addicted to BAD SUGAR you believe that you need BAD SUGAR again and again and again just to keep feeling "OK".

But actually you never quite get back to real contentment – real "OK". Look again at the diagram in Chapter 4. Every time you give your body a stimulant, it develops a tolerance against it. So every time you consume sugar, you need to consume more to get the same boost, and every time you stop, you sink lower. The longer you go on trying to satisfy the Little Monster with sugar, the lower your sense of wellbeing sinks and the more dependent you feel on the stimulant.

This is why eating BAD SUGAR foods never ever makes you feel satisfied.

The Big Monster tells you that BAD SUGAR is the only thing

that can fill the void. However, BAD SUGAR creates a void that is a triple low: a slight physical low, a psychological craving and the misery of being an addict. This triple low becomes your new idea of normal; your new "OK".

While the Little Monster is barely perceptible, the Big Monster really can make you miserable. When it is awakened, it fills your head with thoughts of deprivation, which in turn creates a feeling of yearning. That, along with all the misinformation you've been fed about BAD SUGAR being a source of pleasure, compels you to get another "fix". The only "pleasure" you get is the mild relief of the withdrawal symptoms and the ending of the dissatisfied and unpleasant condition that is created by the belief that BAD SUGAR provides some kind of pleasure or benefit.

ACCEPTANCE

Sugar addiction has nothing to do with your personality and everything to do with the brainwashing you've been subjected to from birth. The craving is nothing more than a desire to feel the way a non-addict feels, but the thought of becoming a non-addict is frightening if you believe that BAD SUGAR gives you pleasure or a crutch. This conflict leaves you feeling helpless and confused. You wish you could just take control of the situation and sort yourself out.

But the hopelessness of the prison makes addicts try to blot out the problem and pretend it doesn't exist. They lie to themselves about the state they're in and laugh it off with other addicts, but deep down you know it's no laughing matter; it's a miserable situation and if you could end it with a wave of a magic wand you would not hesitate.

It's time to release yourself from the prison. Take your head out of the sand and see things as they really are. The beautiful truth is that you don't need a magic wand, but you have something in your hands that's just as effective when it comes to curing addiction: Easyway. All you have to do is follow all the instructions.

TENTH INSTRUCTION: IGNORE ALL ADVICE AND INFLUENCES THAT CONFLICT WITH EASYWAY

You have already taken a big step. You have overcome denial and accepted that you have a BAD SUGAR problem. You have also taken action to do something about the problem. That's another big step. Now all you have to do is kill the Big Monster. Once the Big Monster is dead, you will find it easy to cut off the supply to the Little Monster and it will die very quickly.

The fabulous news is that you have already begun to kill the Big Monster and you understand that the way to finish it off is to see through the illusion of pleasure. The illusion of pleasure is created by brainwashing, which we go through life without questioning. We are brainwashed by parents, friends, role models, the food industry, the medical profession, governments and other so-called "experts", all of whom were themselves brainwashed by other influences of their own. Some of us are brainwashed more than others but all BAD SUGAR addicts are in the same trap and there is only one way out, which is the same for everybody:

UNDO THE BRAINWASHING AND STOP CONSUMING BAD SUGAR!

At this stage, a lot of people say they understand everything I've said completely and are in a hurry to get to the end, but it often turns out that they still retain some belief in the pleasure aspects of BAD SUGAR. As long as you remain a victim of the illusion of pleasure you will always be susceptible to feeling deprived. It's essential, therefore, that we make sure you accept that there is no pleasure and start trusting your instincts.

SUMMARY

- The addictive personality gene theory just gives the addict an excuse to avoid even trying to escape.

- The personality traits shared by addicts are caused by their addiction, they are not the cause of the addiction.

- When you see through the illusion of pleasure you don't need to make excuses.

- Kill the Big Monster and the Little Monster quickly follows.

CHAPTER 12

SEE THROUGH THE ILLUSION

IN THIS CHAPTER

•*TRUST YOUR SENSES* •*A MARGIN FOR ERROR*

•*THE MYTH OF VARIETY* •*WHEN TO EAT*

•*WHEN TO STOP EATING* •*FALSE HUNGER*

You only need to look at the evidence of millions of years of evolution to see that the way we are currently conditioned to eat goes against nature.

Nature's Larder is incredibly complex. What is food for one species is poison for another. Nature has provided a vast menu of options to cater for all species and to ensure that the competition for food isn't too fierce. So how does each species know which items to eat and which to avoid?

Watch an animal approach food and the answer becomes obvious. First, it sees the food and approaches with caution. On reaching the food it will sniff at it, then touch it tentatively. Finally, if its sight, smell and touch are satisfied, it will taste the food. In other words, it uses its senses.

The senses of sight, touch, smell and taste are all an animal needs to distinguish between food and poison; intellect plays no part. It's an ingenious system and it works like a dream. So why shouldn't it work for us?

By now, you should be starting to accept that nature did provide us with exactly the same facility. We recoil if something looks, smells, feels or tastes like poison. Take coffee, for example. A child will be repelled by the taste of coffee. It's only through forcing yourself to build an immunity to the poison that you develop a "taste" for it. As you now know, it's actually a *loss* of taste that enables you to keep drinking it. The same is true of alcohol and cigarettes. Most of us are too young when we first consume sugar to recall our reaction, but people who are not addicted to sugar do recoil at excessive sweetness. BAD SUGAR attempts to mimic the sweetness of fresh, nutritious fruit. Initially, this is the only reason we are remotely attracted to it.

The only reason we continue to consume these poisons is because we are brainwashed into seeing them as a pleasure and we become addicted to them. It is not our senses we are trying to satisfy; it's the Little Monster. Strip away the brainwashing and the truth is plain to see:

THE FOODS THAT TASTE BEST FOR YOU
ARE THE BEST FOR YOU

You don't need labels and sell-by dates to tell you when an apple has turned to poison. The brown, wrinkled skin, the odd smell and mushy feel are all the warning you need.

Instinct is the result of millions of years of natural logic; it is the greatest knowledge there is. With such an ingenious system at your disposal, **WHY WOULD YOU DO ANYTHING OTHER THAN TRUST YOUR SENSES**.

That's what animals do and they don't have the eating problems humans have. We allow intellect to override instinct when we think the intellectual argument has the logical advantage. You should now be able to understand that true logic is in perfect accord with your instinct. Your body was not created by human intellect; it was created by nature and it's nature that provides the most authoritative guide as to what is good for it. When you can see the simple truth that the foods that make you fit and healthy are also the foods that taste the best, you remove the fear of success and thus remove the conflict that creates the tug-of-war.

YOUR SECOND LINE OF DEFENCE

If you did happen to swallow something poisonous, your next level of natural defence would kick in. You would be sick. Your digestive system will do everything it can to expel poison and it will leave you vowing never to make the same mistake again. How often have you heard someone who's overindulged on alcohol say, "I'm never going to drink again"? What they're experiencing is another natural defence: programming by experience. Once you've been poisoned by a substance, your whole body pulls together to deter you from consuming that substance again.

A MARGIN FOR ERROR

In Chapter 8, we listed the foods that we are designed to enjoy in their natural state:

- Fruit
- Vegetables
- Nuts and seeds.

By Nature's design, these are also the foods that are best for us. You may well be thinking, "If I have to restrict my diet to fruit, vegetables, nuts, and seeds, I'm not sure I want to follow this method." Please rest assured, we are not telling you that you have to restrict yourself to these foods.

The aim of this book is to help you enjoy eating and to achieve a new level of happiness. It is not a diet; it does not set out to restrict you. Fruit, vegetables, nuts and seeds are our primary foods and you should make them the basis of your regular diet, but nature has given us secondary foods, a margin for error, which still provide us with the nutrients we need, but not as efficiently. You can add these to your menu, but always keep in touch with your instincts. Ask yourself how much these secondary foods appeal to your senses as you eat them. You will quickly notice how instinct draws you back to your primary foods in preference over anything else.

Look at it, smell it. Would you eat it raw? If you would, the chances are that it is a natural healthy food. If you wouldn't then you need to identify whether it is a secondary food or poison. The more processed the food, the more likely it is to be poison, i.e. to contain BAD SUGAR. Virtually every ready meal or ready-made sauce is packed full of BAD SUGAR. The ingredient list alone will confirm that, but so does the degree of processing it goes through before it reaches your plate.

No doubt, you're wondering about meat. And although there is no doubt that the human race can survive in rude health on a raw vegan diet, if you want to carry on consuming meat then I'd certainly class it as a secondary food. Most meat requires very little processing. Often a simple, swift cooking process is all that is required to make it palatable to you. But it's important to move away from huge portions of meat. Make it a small part of your meal, not the main feature.

The food industry has taken advantage of our ability to adapt to secondary foods to widen its product inventory and thus increase its profit potential. It has bombarded us with advertisements designed to convince us that these foods are what we most want to eat. Mankind's weight problems can be explained by this simple fact: thanks to our intellect and the ability it gives us to spread misinformation, our margin for error has become the norm and the foods that were designed for us have become secondary.

Our objective now is to use our intellect to reverse that process by seeing things as they really are: in other words, rebuilding the image of our genuine favourite foods by seeing through the illusions and by replacing myths with the truth. You will know when you are following the truth and not an illusion because you will feel genuine enjoyment and wellbeing every time you eat.

THE MYTH OF VARIETY

The fear of success is based on the myth that a healthy diet has to be a boring, unvaried diet. Let's look more closely at just how varied the human diet is.

Supermarkets stock thousands of different lines. The impression, therefore, is that we demand huge variety in our diet and that is exactly the impression the food industry wants to create. The broader the marketplace, the bigger the market. But think about your place within that market. Take the cereal aisle, for example. There are dozens of different breakfast cereals available, but do you pick a different one each time? Do you play the field, or do you pick your favourites time after time after time?

Smokers are the same. There are dozens of cigarette brands available, but every smoker will buy his or her favourite brand every time. If they can't get it in their usual shop, they will go out of their way to find a shop where they can.

ADDICTS AREN'T INTERESTED IN VARIETY, THEY JUST THINK THEY ARE

If you really are worried about variety, take a look at the fruit and veg section of your local supermarket. You will find it offers more variety than any other. And if you examine the average diet of even unhealthy eaters, you will find that most of the variety is provided by our primary foods. The typical dinner plate will comprise one type of meat and three types of vegetable. We generally choose our meat from four options: chicken, pork, beef or lamb; whereas our vegetables might be peas, carrots, green beans, onions, lettuce, tomatoes, cabbage, spinach, broccoli... the list goes on and on.

When it comes to cakes and biscuits you're looking at three basic ingredients: butter, flour and sugar; each of which is relatively bland in flavour. By cutting them out of your diet you will lose nothing in terms of variety or interest. In fact, you will lose nothing at all. The only reason you continue to eat these bland, sugary foods is to satisfy the Little Monster.

WHEN TO EAT

Just as our instinct regarding what to eat has been confused by brainwashing, so too has the instinct of when to eat. Let's go back to the reason why we eat, as discussed in Chapter 8. Not boredom, nor comfort, nor routine, but rather the real reason we eat is to provide our body with the nutrients it needs. The signal that tells us when we need to do that is **HUNGER.**

Hunger is like the fuel gauge on a car. It increases as our resources of fuel decrease. Now think about how and when you put fuel in your car. Do you put the same amount of fuel in at the same time of day every day, regardless of how much fuel you've used? If you did there would come a time when you're sloshing fuel all over the forecourt.

But this is how we fuel ourselves. We sit down to dinner at around the same time every evening and eat roughly the same amount of food every day, regardless of how hungry we feel. The equivalent of all that fuel sloshing across the forecourt is the excess fat that gets stored in different parts of your body, impairing the way you function and the way you feel.

Presumably, you're more sensible than to try and fill your car when it's already full. Instead, you go by the fuel gauge. But how far do you let the gauge fall before you stop to add fuel? As soon as it dips below full? More likely you'll let it get below a quarter full before you start looking for a petrol station.

Hunger is nature's signal to us that it is time to refuel, but we have already explained that the longer we go hungry, the better the food will taste and the more pleasure we will get from eating. If you eat at the first sign of hunger, you will never get the full enjoyment from a meal. So when exactly should you satisfy your hunger?

Think of hunger as a fuel gauge numbered from 0 to 20, where 0 is empty and 20 is full up. On this gauge, 10 is the point at which hunger is satisfied, the range between 7 and 10 is slight hunger and the range between 3 and 7 is true hunger. When the needle drops to true hunger, that is when you should be looking to eat. You may feel the first hint of hunger as the needle hovers between 7 and 10, but don't take this as a sign to eat at once, otherwise you will not get the full pleasure from the food. The hunger you feel at this point on the gauge is not painful or bad; that

only happens when you reach 0 and stay there for some time. If your mind is occupied with other things, you probably won't even feel it.

If you feel slight hunger and somebody starts talking to you about the lovely meal they ate in a restaurant the previous evening, it will make you feel more hungry than you really are. Slight hunger can be enhanced by exposing you to the smell of food, or the sight of it. Beware! This is a trick used by the food industry to make you think you want food when you don't.

Recognizing your own different levels of hunger is key to solving your eating problem. Just as advertisements can suggest that you are hungrier than you really are, you can reverse the process and see that what you think is true hunger, may only be slight hunger. If you can focus on something else, it may disappear completely. If you do feel it, see it as a sign that you are heading towards another enjoyable meal and take pleasure in feeling it grow, knowing that the more it grows, the better the meal will taste.

This is not deprivation. In fact, it's the opposite. You are guaranteeing yourself pleasure. You're lucky enough to have a ready supply of food available whenever you need it. Unlike wild animals, you don't have to risk life and limb going out to get it. Neither are you a victim of famine. Starvation is not your problem. In fact, your problem is the complete opposite. All you have to do is rely on nature's fuel gauge and every meal you eat will be an enjoyable experience.

Don't misunderstand me, make sure that you plan well for each meal that you intend to eat. The most common reason for someone reaching for quick, poisonous, addictive junk food is lack of planning. It's so easy to make a bad decision because you haven't shopped for dinner or decided what you intend to eat before entering the restaurant.

WHEN TO STOP

Knowing when to eat is key to your enjoyment of eating; knowing when to stop is key to your enjoyment of life.

With a car, the norm is either to keep filling until the tank is full or to put in fuel to a certain value. Having a full tank may give you a feeling of reassurance but is it going to get the best performance out of your car? The more fuel you put in, the heavier the car becomes and, therefore, the less economical it is to run. Ask any Formula One technician. When they fuel up a racing car, they make careful calculations that enable them to put in the exact amount of fuel required to keep the car running for the required distance and no more. That way they keep the weight to a minimum and the car runs faster.

With nature's fuel gauge, you really don't have to make those calculations; the gauge does it for you.

The range from 3 to 7 is true hunger; this is the time to start eating. Between 7 and 10 is slight hunger; the time when hunger is often imperceptible and eating will not give the same amount of pleasure. At 10, hunger is satisfied; this is the time to stop eating. If you keep eating until the gauge reaches 20, you will be completely full up.

> Eat slowly to give your body time to register that it has received the nutrients it requires. Chew the food properly. If you bolt the food down, you will still be feeling hungry when you have eaten enough to satisfy and will end up overeating.

Continuing to eat beyond the point of satisfaction is what leaves us feeling bloated and spoils the enjoyment of the meal. So why doesn't nature's fuel gauge send us a signal to stop?

The truth of the matter is that it does. Just as increased hunger makes food taste better, overeating can literally leave a bad taste in the mouth. Nature has designed us so that the desire to eat and the pleasure of eating cut off when we are satisfied. The problem is that we have been conditioned to disregard these signals.

The amazing thing about BAD SUGAR food, whether it's chocolate, sweets, bread, pasta, pastries, or rice is that they are so nutritionally bankrupt that our instincts don't recognize them as food. This is why we have a tendency to eat the whole box of chocolates, or the entire pack of biscuits, or a huge bowl of pasta to the point where we feel absolutely stuffed, bloated, guilt-ridden and sick. Never having to experience those awful feelings again is priceless.

Such is the constant bombardment of mixed messages about what we should be eating, we've forgotten how to recognize the messages from our own natural gauge. Embrace hunger as your friend, not as something to be averted immediately you feel it. You will then start to recognize the signals that tell you when to stop eating.

Rest assured, recognizing these signals is far more simple than it sounds. Nature's fuel gauge does the work for you. Once you've taken in the nutrients your body needs, it will register "satisfied" and your desire to keep eating will end.

This is a simple response that you are already well practised at utilizing. When you drink a glass of water, you stop drinking when your thirst is quenched, not when your belly is full. When you eat the right foods, you will find the same applies to eating.

If the food you take in does not contain the nutrients your body requires, however, the gauge will not register "satisfied" and the only thing that will stop you eating is when you can physically take no more. When you regularly eat foods that do not contain the required nutrients, overeating becomes the norm. It is important that you remember this fact: **LACK OF NUTRIENTS LEADS TO OVEREATING.**

FALSE HUNGER AND "PEAK JUNK"

The cries of the Little Monster feel like mild hunger. It is a slightly empty and slightly insecure feeling that is almost imperceptible. But this feeling has nothing to do with hunger. It is all to do with BAD SUGAR addiction. Until you get your next fix of BAD SUGAR, it remains.

It's the same for a smoker craving the next cigarette, an alcoholic craving the next drink, a heroin addict craving the next fix. When you believe that the only thing that will satisfy that craving is the very thing that caused it in the first place, the discomfort will intensify until you get your fix. But it's not the physical withdrawal feeling that gets worse. The worsening sensations are physical, but they are caused by a mental process… of wanting something but not being able to have it.

When you know and understand that BAD SUGAR doesn't relieve the discomfort, but in fact causes it and perpetuates it, the physical withdrawal is hardly noticeable and becoming free becomes not only easy, but enjoyable.

If you respond to false hunger by eating sugar you will temporarily relieve the symptom, creating the impression that the sugar has satisfied your hunger. In reality, all you have done is ensure that the false hunger will return and you will need to take in more BAD SUGAR each time to get any sense of relief. Remember, with addiction the tendency is always to take more.

BAD SUGAR never satisfies genuine hunger because it is "empty carbs", i.e. it contains none of the nutrients your body needs. If you try to satisfy genuine hunger by eating empty carbs you will keep eating until you can physically take no more. This is why we are witnessing a global epidemic of obesity and diabetes. Our consumption of BAD SUGAR, almost to the exclusion of anything else, is inflicting a calamity of biblical proportions on mankind as junk has begun to make up a greater and greater proportion of our intake. As a species, we've reached "PEAK JUNK"! The human body simply can't take the levels of BAD SUGAR with which it is being constantly bombarded.

Once you understand the difference between real and false hunger – and you see that only by eating the right type of foods you can avoid false hunger – you will truly be able to satisfy real hunger and get the maximum enjoyment from eating and living.

SUMMARY

- **Your senses are designed to distinguish between food and poison.**

- **Foods that taste the best are the best for you.**

- **You can eat secondary foods, but be wary of making them the norm or the main feature of your meal.**

- **Eat according to your natural fuel gauge and food will taste better.**

- **The false hunger created by BAD SUGAR addiction can only be ended by quitting BAD SUGAR.**

CHAPTER 13

YOUR FAVOURITE FOOD

IN THIS CHAPTER
- *WHAT'S THE CATCH?*
- *NATURAL EVIDENCE* - *NUTRITIONAL EVIDENCE*
- *READY TO TAKE CONTROL*

Throughout this book I have used the phrase "your favourite food" and promised that by the end you will be able to eat as much of your favourite food as you want, whenever you want and as often as you want, and be the exact weight you want to be, without having to diet or undergo special exercise or having to use willpower or gimmicks and without feeling miserable or deprived.

You may have gained the impression that this was a play on words, that I was merely twisting the sense of the phrase to suit the purpose of Easyway.

It is true that, for the method to be successful, your definition of "your favourite food" must change between the start of the book and the finish, but this is no con trick on the part of Easyway. On the contrary, I am just helping you to see through the con trick that has made you a slave to sugar.

Remember what you have learned about illusions: once you

see the truth, you can never be fooled by the illusion again. That is how you know that the food industry has been brainwashing you, and Easyway is showing you how things really are. If you're unsure about this, go back and re-read Chapter 7.

Remember too why the refined sugar industry grew up: to sell us a product that entices us into eating secondary foods by replicating the sweetness of fruit. As the market expanded and the sales pitch became more and more persuasive, we became brainwashed into believing that these secondary foods were our favourites. Unlike naturally healthy foods, processed carbs and starchy carbs are indigestible, flavourless and unappealing in their raw form. No wonder we're in such a mess.

If you still have any doubts that fruit, salads and vegetables are mankind's favourite foods or you think you'd prefer a cream cake or a chocolate biscuit, it means you have not yet fully seen through the illusion. Let's take a closer look at the facts.

UNBRAINWASHED TASTES

We can learn a lot about our natural instincts by observing the behaviour of our young. When a baby is born the first thing it wants to satisfy its hunger is its mother's milk. The desire is instinctive. It is nature's way of making sure the baby is drawn to the very best food it can find for its own needs.

As the baby grows older and is weaned off milk and on to solids, its next instinctive desire is for fruit. The baby food manufacturers have come up with all sorts of concoctions to sell in those little jars that adorn the supermarket shelves, but it's always the puréed fruit that babies eat most readily. The ones containing chicken and other meats are an acquired taste. Sadly those fruit pots often contain huge amounts of BAD SUGAR and, as a result of processing, deliver unnatural levels of sugar to the infant.

Even as toddlers and young children we favour fruit over other types of food. Indeed, throughout our lives our favourite foods are those flavoured with fruit. All those puddings, cakes and confectionery that you regard as irresistible, how good would they taste without flavouring? And while you think about that, how good would they taste if they were flavoured with chicken or beef? Can you imagine taking a bite of a cream cake that tasted of beef? You'd spit it out immediately. Of course we mainly use those kind of flavourings to add taste to processed and starchy carbs: savoury pies, pasta and potato crisps.

We give taste to the sweet items, which would otherwise be bland, by adding lemon, strawberry, blueberry, cherry, vanilla, almond and so on. All of these are flavours extracted from fruits, nuts and seeds.

When it comes to flavouring drinks, we always turn to fruit: blackcurrant, orange, lemon, lime, strawberry, raspberry, peach, pineapple, banana, mango and cranberry. And not just soft drinks either – in addition to the grapes and hops that go into wine and beer, we flavour spirits with juniper, sloe, orange, lemon, cherry, apricot and more.

It is beyond dispute that fruit appeals to our taste buds more than any other type of food, and for one very good reason: Nature designed it that way because fruit is also the best source of all the nutrients we need.

Just as we can learn a lot by observing our own young, we can also learn from our closest relative in the animal kingdom, the chimpanzee. The chimpanzee shares 98 per cent of our DNA and, like man, is an omnivore. It eats both plants and meat. But its favourite food by far is fruit. About 60 per cent of a chimp's diet is fruit, while only about 5 per cent is meat and insects.

Studies have found that male chimps use meat they have killed as a gift to demonstrate their prowess. Given the choice, a chimpanzee would much rather eat fruit and leaves.

Now, do you ever look at a chimpanzee and question whether it is getting enough variety in its diet, or whether it is getting the necessary vitamins and minerals? This is an animal that is infinitely stronger and infinitely faster than we are, has boundless energy and doesn't suffer with weight problems or any of the eating disorders that have come to blight mankind. For an animal that is so closely related to us, doesn't that make you think?

Next time you hear a nutritionist or doctor spouting confused opinions about whether or not your diet is lacking in certain nutrients or foods, particularly starchy carbs, remember the chimpanzee. There is no clearer indication of Nature's Guide. Remember the entire animal kingdom, how each and every species of animal, excluding the animals whose diets we dictated or contaminated, are perfect specimens of fitness, health, and physique. Even the animals that appear overweight to us – say, elephants, hippopotamuses, or walruses – are just the size and shape that they need to be in order to survive and flourish.

Think of antelope, lions, tigers, apes, wolves, gorillas, eagles. All are immeasurably stronger, more powerful and faster than mankind. Even small animals are superfit titans compared to modern man. Among the same species, body shape, muscle definition, and physique barely differ. They don't work out or jog or pump iron. What else do they all have in common? They don't, in their natural habitat, consume refined sugar or processed carbs or starchy carbs. They are entirely "BAD SUGAR–FREE".

TUTTI FRUTTI

Amongst a multitude of options, fruit is the food that the chimp prefers to eat. And when you look at all the evidence, it's clear that fruit is what we prefer to eat too. It ticks all the boxes of Nature's Guide for humankind.

Speed and ease

You don't have to chase fruit and it doesn't fight back. It requires no preparation and is easy to digest, so it doesn't use up energy as you extract the nutrients, nor does it leave waste that you can't easily dispose of.

Nutrition

Fruit contains all the vitamins and minerals you need to grow healthy and strong, and they are extracted quickly, reducing the time lag between consuming enough and your gauge registering "satisfied", and thus avoiding the susceptibility to overeating.

Water

Fruit consists mainly of water, the most vital nutrient for man. Without water we quickly die, but fruit provides us with a way to carry water around in solid form.

Cool

Unlike other foods, fruit remains cool in hot weather, so it quenches your thirst and satisfies your hunger at the same time.

Taste and variety

Fruit tastes great without any special preparation. It is the food we prefer to eat as infants, before the brainwashing kicks in, and it provides our favourite flavours throughout life. In fact, it provides an abundance of flavours.

Unlike the many different cereals, biscuits or chocolate bars available in the shops, each type of fruit has its own distinct taste, which we can readily identify.

Spend a moment to consider this list and imagine the flavour of each:

- Apple
- Pear
- Peach
- Banana
- Pineapple
- Plum
- Orange
- Grape

- Satsuma
- Melon
- Mango
- Apricot
- Cherry
- Kiwi
- Pomegranate
- Strawberry
- Raspberry
- Blackberry
- Blueberry
- Blackcurrant
- Redcurrant

THE AFFORDABILITY MYTH

While we're on the subject of shopping, it's worth considering another of the chief concerns of modern life: money. There is a myth that eating good-quality, healthy food costs more than eating junk. Next time you're feeling peckish and you fancy a snack, pay close attention to the prices. For the price of a chocolate bar you could buy two apples. For the price of a small cake you could buy five or six! Carry out your own comparison next time you're out shopping. It will dispel any thoughts about fruit being the expensive option once and for all.

READY TO SHELVE BAD SUGAR

Despite all the brainwashing, we know deep down that fruit is good for us and BAD SUGAR is bad for us. When someone is ill and needs to recuperate, what do you give them to eat, fresh fruit or cake and sweets?

We've been brainwashed into believing that BAD SUGAR gives us some sort of pleasure or crutch. We're caught in a tug-of-war; fear of what will happen if we carry on consuming BAD SUGAR against fear of what will happen if we stop; how will we cope without that perceived pleasure or crutch?

The way to win the tug-of-war and cure your BAD SUGAR addiction is to remove your craving for BAD SUGAR.

The craving is caused by eating and drinking BAD SUGAR. Therefore, the way to cure your addiction is to stop consuming BAD SUGAR: to kill the Little Monster. The only way to do that easily and permanently is to remove the desire: that means killing the Big Monster.

By now you should be feeling the Big Monster beginning to die. It is a simple process of opening your mind to the truth. Once you can see the truth, the illusions no longer work. The evidence we have presented is not Easyway evidence; it is the evidence of naturalists and nutritionists who have observed the world we live in and reported what they have studied. You could gather this evidence yourself from readily available sources.

The only reason there is any doubt over our favourite foods is because the food industry has done everything in its power to brainwash us into thinking otherwise.

Had it not done so, and had we not swallowed the misinformation, the food industry would be a fraction of its current size.

There are huge vested interests in keeping you addicted to BAD SUGAR. It's important that you realize that what you have always regarded as a preference is actually no choice at all. You had no say the first time you consumed refined sugar, processed carbs, and starchy carbs and you have been brainwashed ever since into believing that BAD SUGAR food is fun, delicious, irresistible, naughty and a guaranteed source of happiness.

Ask yourself why you're reading this book and you will quickly confirm that it is quite the opposite. You understand now that BAD SUGAR foods and drinks offer you nothing in terms of nutrition, nor in terms of taste. The taste you associate with BAD SUGAR foods comes from fruit or vegetables, our genuine favourite foods.

You also understand that the only reason you think you get pleasure or a crutch from eating sugary foods is because you are addicted to sugar.

The "pleasure" is nothing more than the temporary relief from the cries of the Little Monster. If you didn't have the Little Monster in the first place, you would have nothing to relieve. It's like deciding to wear tight shoes all day, just for the relief of taking them off.

You are ready now to finish reversing the brainwashing and take control of the way you eat. First, though, there is one more red herring that we need to cover: the sugar alternative.

SUMMARY

- Before we are brainwashed, fruit is the food we are drawn to.
- Fruit is the preferred food of our closest relation, the chimpanzee.
- Fruit and vegetables tick all the boxes of Nature's Guide.
- Fruit and vegetables provide all our favourite flavours.
- Fruit and vegetables are the easiest food for us to digest.
- Fruit and vegetables give us an energy surplus.

Chapter 14

SUBSTITUTES

Perhaps you think you can solve your problem by finding an alternative that gives you the sweetness of sugar without the calories. This won't cure your addiction. In fact, it will force you deeper into the trap.

The food industry has unearthed another vast marketing opportunity in "diet" versions of all sorts of food and drink. These "diet" versions use artificial sweeteners to provide the sweetness you crave without giving you the calories. Hence, they should help you lose weight.

That's the theory anyway. In reality it's nonsense. For a start, the term "artificial sweetener", as an alternative to sugar, implies that sugar is natural. Incredibly there have been cases where the sugar industry has sued manufacturers of artificial sweeteners for implying that their product is more natural than it is. As if the sugar industry has a leg to stand on! Sugar may originate from a natural source, but by the time it's been processed there is nothing natural about it.

So let's make no mistake about the name: any substance that is added to intensify the sweetness of food or drink is an artificial sweetener. And that includes sugar.

What you have to ask yourself is why you would want to make any food sweeter than it already is. One reason would be to make an otherwise bland food more appealing. The other would be because you have an addiction that makes you think you get some form of pleasure or crutch from sugary foods.

THE SUBSTITUTE THEORY

When it comes to curing a sugar addiction, you may be led to believe that substituting sugar with other artificial sweeteners can help. A popular theory for curing any addiction is that it helps to tackle the problem in two parts: the physical part and the psychological part. To illustrate how the substitute theory is supposed to work, and why it doesn't work, a good example is nicotine addiction.

Doctors who are trying to help patients quit smoking will prescribe some form of nicotine replacement therapy (NRT), usually in the form of a patch or chewing gum. A better name for it would be nicotine maintenance treatment. It's the same approach that the tobacco industry is using to keep everybody hooked.

The treatment is based on the theory that the hardest thing about quitting smoking is coping with the physical withdrawal. This is made even harder, the theory says, if you are also having to break your smoking habit at the same time, by which they mean the ritual of buying cigarettes, unwrapping the packet, lighting the cigarette, feeling it in your hand, standing outside the office in the rain.

If you can continue to take nicotine via some alternative source, you can first concentrate on breaking the "habit" without the constant distraction of withdrawal and without the harmful toxins from cigarette smoke. Once you've broken the "habit", you can then tackle the physical withdrawal, reducing your nicotine intake bit by bit until you are completely free.

It sounds quite straightforward, doesn't it? But NRT has been an abject failure. Just like the e-cigarettes and other alternatives peddled by the tobacco industry and pharmaceutical industry, the NRT solutions recommended by the medical profession serve only to keep smokers hooked on nicotine. The great irony of NRT solutions is that they actually enable smokers to get nicotine at times when they would otherwise make do without it, such as on flights and in restaurants. Far from being the key to their prison, NRT keeps them more firmly locked in. They often end up consuming more nicotine rather than less, and even worse, they continue to smoke at a level that leaves them seriously exposed to the horrific illnesses and diseases caused by smoking. It's the worst of all worlds.

FLAWED LOGIC

There are two fatal flaws in the substitute theory that explain why it fails:

1. It's not habit, it's addiction.

2. The physical addiction is easy to break. Addiction is 99 per cent mental.

Smokers think the ritual they go through is part of the enjoyment they get from smoking. They are brainwashed into believing that it's a habit they've got into. The truth is the only reason they go through that ritual is to get the nicotine and the belief that it gives them some sort of pleasure or crutch is purely the Big Monster.

Do you like injections? Most people don't. Even the more resolute among us who can watch the needle going in without wincing would never say they actually get pleasure from it. But heroin addicts can't wait for the needle to pierce the skin. Heroin addicts don't enjoy the ritual of injecting themselves. They're just doing it to get the drug to which they're addicted. They are under no illusions that there is genuine pleasure in it; it's just the temporary respite from a condition of dissatisfaction caused by the drug. The drug doesn't relieve that feeling; it causes it.

Substitutes don't help the smoker stop craving nicotine and they won't help you stop craving sugar either. Whatever means you use to add artificial sweetness to food and drink, it will only serve to keep the Big Monster alive. Consuming BAD SUGAR foods and drinks is not a habit, it's an addiction and to cure any addiction you have to kill both monsters.

Which brings us on to the second flaw in the substitute theory: the assumption that the biggest obstacle to quitting is the physical withdrawal. The theory assumes that the physical pangs of withdrawal are so severe that they need to be tackled gradually by reducing your intake little by little, and without any other distractions. When you understand the nature of addiction, you know that the tendency is always to crave more, not less. By gradually reducing your intake, you actually make quitting harder.

As any smoker who has quit with Easyway will tell you, the physical pangs of withdrawal are so slight as to be almost imperceptible and they disappear within a few days. These pangs are the death throes of the Little Monster and when you know they mean an end to your slavery to nicotine, they actually become a source of pleasure.

Killing the Little Monster is easy: simply deny it its fix and it will die very quickly. You don't have to give it all your concentration or apply any willpower. Killing the Little Monster is only hard if you fail to destroy the Big Monster. It is the Big Monster that causes you to feel deprived and miserable if you can't have your fix.

It's not the "habit" of consuming BAD SUGAR foods and drinks that you need to break before you kill the Little Monster, it's the desire. If you fail to remove the desire for BAD SUGAR you may be able to will yourself to abstain for long enough to kill the Little Monster, but other triggers such as hunger or stress will stir the Big Monster into making you think, "I want sugar."

For the addict who has been through cold turkey, this is devastating. You think you've killed the Little Monster but suddenly there you are craving your fix again. This is only a problem for addicts who don't understand the nature of the trap they are in. With Easyway, you remove the desire before you kill the Little Monster.

A HEALTHY ALTERNATIVE?

Our desire for sweetness is a natural predisposition designed to draw us to the food that is best for us: fruit. Anything that attempts to substitute the sweetness of fruit with processed alternatives is in conflict with Nature's Guide.

Sweeteners are sold as a calorie-free alternative to refined sugar, but they can have an adverse effect on your eating in other ways. The hormone leptin helps to regulate your appetite and helps your body to metabolize. Aspartame and other sweeteners are acids, which have been found to lower the leptin in your body by as much as 35 per cent. This has a catastrophic effect on your ability to gauge hunger and on your body's ability to metabolize efficiently.

Another alternative is powdered fructose, sometimes sold as "fruit sugar". Don't confuse this with the natural fructose in fruit. The process of extracting it from the fruit, separating it from the water, fibre and other nutrients, leaves an empty substance just like refined sugar, which acts on your body in exactly the same way.

Remember too that drinks contain artificial sweeteners. Alcohol, fizzy drinks, cordials and processed fruit juices are all catering for a craving for excess sweetness, created by the consumption of BAD SUGAR.

Research into the safety of artificial sweeteners has

already thrown up enough evidence to suggest that these substances cannot be assumed to be harmless. There is still a lot of work to be done before we really know the effect that these substances have on our bodies. They could well turn out to be even more harmful than sugar.

SLAVERY

One of the arguments the doctors use to promote nicotine substitutes is that, even if they don't break your nicotine addiction, at least they don't fill you with all the other harmful poisons associated with smoking. In other words, their method for getting you off one set of poisons is to keep you hooked on another.

You can see the parallel with "artificial sweeteners": supposedly they give you the sweetness you crave without the harmful calories. In fact, many of these sweeteners may be more harmful, but this is not the reason the theory is flawed.

The number one reason why any smoker wants to quit is to get free from the slavery of nicotine addiction. There are many other reasons for wanting to quit: health, money, cleanliness, to name but three, but the thing that makes smokers miserable when they fail to quit is the feeling of frustration and helplessness that comes from being a slave to nicotine. Otherwise strong people, who are used to getting their way in life, find themselves incapable of breaking free from the nicotine trap.

The same is true of BAD SUGAR addiction. Being overweight or fearing that you might become diabetic is not a happy state of mind, but the real misery of the addiction comes from the frustration and loss of self-respect and self-esteem that you feel when you just realize that you're simply not in control.

BY USING SUBSTITUTES YOU CONSIGN YOURSELF TO A LIFETIME OF SLAVERY

TRADING ADDICTIONS

Some smokers who quit with the willpower method reward themselves for their sacrifice by turning to other substitutes, such as sweets and chocolate. The same happens in reverse. People who want to diet will take up smoking, under the false belief that nicotine makes you thin, and they come to regard the cigarette as their reward for abstaining from sugar. The fact is that they end up with yet another problem. They become addicted to nicotine and remain addicted to BAD SUGAR.

The great evil of all substitutes, whatever they may be, is that they perpetuate the illusion that you're making a sacrifice when you quit.

At the start of the chapter we posed a question:

WHY WOULD YOU WANT TO MAKE ANY FOOD SWEETER THAN IT ALREADY IS?

We are surrounded by an abundance of natural food that tastes wonderful and is good for us without the need for any human intervention. We also have a ready supply of a drink that is refreshing, thirst-quenching, highly nutritious and falls from the sky. Why create second-rate food, which tastes so bland that we have to add other artificial substances to it? Surely that should be the last resort, not your favourite way of eating. The only reason we don't see this as strange is because we have been brainwashed into believing that it is normal. In other words, there is only one reason why you would want to intensify the sweetness of any food or drink: **ADDICTION**.

When you see through the illusion, you'll want a way of eating that's completely free from artificial sweetness. There is an easy way to achieve that: **QUIT! IT'S THE <u>ONLY</u> ALTERNATIVE!**

---------------------- **SUMMARY** -----------------

- **Your sugar problem is not habit; it's addiction.**
- **Addiction is 1 per cent physical and 99 per cent mental.**
- **Substitutes perpetuate the illusion that you're making a sacrifice when you quit.**
- **Choosing to remain a BAD SUGAR addict is like choosing to wear tight shoes just for the relief of taking them off.**
- **Don't assume that artificial sweeteners are not harmful to your health or that they might help you to freedom.**
- **There is only one reason for intensifying the sweetness of any food or drink, and that's addiction.**

CHAPTER 15

REVERSE THE BRAINWASHING

IN THIS CHAPTER
• BE SELFISH FOR ONCE • A TWO-PRONGED ATTACK
• DEPRIVATION • A NEW STATE OF MIND
• THE ELEVENTH INSTRUCTION

The time has come to start reversing the effects of all that brainwashing and see good and bad foods as they really are.

The food industry is like a runaway train that has gone down the wrong track. It is so huge and has gathered so much momentum that nobody has the power to stop it. So you might be wondering how it can possibly be easy to reverse the brainwashing in the face of such an irresistible force. The answer is simple: **DO IT FOR YOURSELF.**

It's not your responsibility to bring the food industry to a halt. That is not our aim. The purpose of this book is to cure your addiction to BAD SUGAR and make you happy about the way you eat. Put everyone else to one side. This is your happiness we're talking about and you are the one person that matters. All the other sugar addicts can take care of themselves. After all, this book is available around the world.

See your task as a direct showdown between you and your addiction. Wouldn't you back yourself every time? All you have to consider is your own position and realize that you have been brainwashed. Once you have accepted that fact, you are well on your way. The next step is to make your mind up to do something about it. The third step is to actually do it.

You have come a long way since you started reading this book. It's safe to assume that you have opened your mind and understood all you have read. The fact that you haven't thrown the book across the room and resigned yourself to a life of unhappy eating proves that you want to see this through. That is crucial. Understanding the logic behind Easyway is no good if it doesn't compel you to take action.

A TWO-PRONGED ATTACK

It's surprisingly simple to reverse the brainwashing. All it requires is for you to keep an open mind and do two things.

The first is to take the time to concentrate on the foods that were designed for you by nature and start seeing them as the wonderful and beneficial packages that they are. Cut open a ripe, juicy, colourful peach, orange, pineapple or pear; breathe in the amazing aroma; feel your mouth watering at the prospect of that delicious flavour; look at the cool, fresh juice; and appreciate the energy and nutrients that your body is going to gain from it, with barely any effort and a minimum of waste.

Try some fruits that you haven't tried before. Explore the wide variety that's readily available in the shops. Exotic fruits like mango, kiwi, passion fruit and pomegranate, or different types of berries. Each one has its own distinct look, smell, feel and flavour, and each one is packed with nutritional goodness and taste.

While you're exploring, try the vast array of fresh, delicious, nutrient-packed, high-water-content vegetables. You can take your pick from carrots, cabbage, lettuce, radish, cauliflower, tomato, pepper, avocado, mushroom, broccoli, spinach and many, many more. They all taste fabulous raw and you can mix them to create delicious, nourishing dishes.

Just by exploring the variety of fresh fruit and vegetables available, your choice of dishes will expand. If you feared that cutting out BAD SUGAR would limit your options when it came to meal times, you can now put that fear to one side.

Your second action point is to take the time to see the foods that you have always believed to be your favourites for what they really are. It doesn't take much imagination to realize how you have been brainwashed into seeing junk food as something special. Analyse the advertisements and ask yourself exactly what they're telling you. Notice the way they skirt around the subject, avoiding the truth by wrapping it in clever wordplay and a concoction of distracting imagery.

The fact is that processed food, which includes anything cooked, tastes bland to us unless it is flavoured with fruit or another of our primary foods. Don't just take our word for it; put it to the test. Try some rice or pasta without any fat, seasoning, or sauce, or a slice of bread without butter, jam or any other filling or topping. Peel and boil a potato. Eat it without any butter or seasoning or sauce. Be completely straight with yourself: how does it actually taste? And how does it compare to that cool, succulent fruit?

NOTHING TO LOSE

By now you should be in full agreement that there is a stark contrast between the genuine enjoyment of eating fruit and the perceived enjoyment of eating BAD SUGAR. It's easy to put it to the test and most people have no difficulty accepting it when they do, yet some people reach this stage and still fear that they are going to feel deprived when they quit.

While they acknowledge that nothing tastes as good as fresh fruit and vegetables, they still fear that they will be missing out in some way if they "give up" BAD SUGAR. Smokers who try to quit using the willpower method experience a similar fear. They worry that they will never be able to concentrate or enjoy a social occasion ever again once they no longer have cigarettes. This is because they haven't understood the nicotine trap. They still believe they are making a sacrifice.

People with eating problems make the same false connections for the same reason. Perhaps you associate cake, biscuits, ice cream and desserts with get-togethers with friends. You may believe that those occasions won't be the same without those "treats". Or you like to buy a chocolate bar on your journey home from work and you fear that the journey will become even more of a drag without the chocolate bar.

Perhaps you see processed and starchy carbs as an important, inexpensive, and hunger satisfying part of your diet? You might be wondering how you might feel "full up" without them. Yet has it occurred to you that the pursuit of feeling "full", especially using foods that have no nutritional value, is pointless as well as being a clear symptom of your addiction?

Maybe you're worried about denying your family these "foods". But would you really wish to feed them food which you now understand to be junk, poisonous and addictive? If a beautiful wild animal – a lion, or chimpanzee, or an antelope – was left in your care would you really ignore its favourite foods according to Nature's Guide and choose to make pasta, potato or rice the main ingredient in its diet?

Why can we see it so clearly in that scenario yet we struggle to apply it to ourselves? Can you see how thoroughly we've been brainwashed into ignoring Nature's Guide?

The fact that we've survived putting the junk into our bodies for so long is testimony to the power and robustness of the human body. Our bodies have worked hard, day after day, year after year, to deal with the junk that we've subjected them to.

How many potatoes do you consume in a week? How much pasta? How much bread? Imagine all those items in your mind. A whole week's worth. Then imagine a whole year's worth of each food item. Strip away the fats and the sauces and the seasoning and imagine tasking your body to process those unnatural, unhealthy, damaging and addictive foods rather than nutritious, healthy, natural fruit and vegetables. Think of it in terms of simply the physical weight, bulk and stodge of those refined sugar, processed and starchy carb "foods". No wonder that eventually our bodies begin to show the strain. In the end we become incapable of handling the poison and that's when our bodies begin to show the signs of the damage we've done.

When you replace all that stodge and poison with delicious, easily digestible fruits and vegetables, it will feel like a huge weight has been lifted from your mind as well as your body.

When we look at the global epidemic of obesity and Type 2 diabetes, even in the poorest countries in the world, and see that these figures coincide with "peak BAD SUGAR consumption", isn't it obvious what has happened?

THE TIDE IS TURNING

People are beginning to set themselves free. Many thousands of people have discovered Type 2 diabetes can be reversed by losing weight and cutting out BAD SUGAR. It's dawning on millions of people that the food companies have got fat on our addiction to BAD SUGAR and that the pharmaceutical industry has got fat prescribing us a lifetime's medication to treat a disease that could be cured by changing our diet and eating our way back to health. **IT'S EXTRAORDINARY THAT THE TWO INDUSTRIES HAVE CONSPIRED: ONE FEEDING US POISON THAT MAKES US ILL, THE OTHER FEEDING US "MEDICINE" THAT ENABLES US TO KEEP EATING THE POISON.**

It's only recently that large parts of the medical profession are beginning to see the truth, and mainstream attitudes to Type 2 diabetes and diet are beginning to change.

IT'S NOT ABOUT THE SUGAR

Some people go to extraordinary lengths to bake cakes and biscuits for gatherings with friends and they pin the success of the occasion on the quality of their baking. Usually, if any social occasion is a happy one it's not because of the food, it's because of the company. Some people mistake the food as the source of happiness because they associate it with the happy occasion.

Take away the people, or replace them with people you don't like, and would the occasion be as happy just because there's cake and biscuits? More likely it would be doubly miserable. Take away the cake and biscuits but keep your favourite people and the occasion will still be a happy one. The fact that you partially relieve your craving for BAD SUGAR on these occasions makes you think it's the BAD SUGAR that has made you happy. It's important that you recognize the difference between genuine and false pleasure.

A false pleasure diminishes the more you come to depend on the stimulant and fools you into thinking you are getting some benefit when, in fact, you are doing yourself untold harm. A genuine pleasure has no downside. It gives sustained happiness and physical benefits. If you can choose between genuine pleasure and false pleasure, doesn't it make sense to pick the one that does you lasting good?

The chocolate bar on your journey home from work is an illusory crutch. You find the journey boring; you get restless and fidgety. The chocolate bar appears to relax you. The act of eating it gives you something to think about for part of the journey and it feels like a pleasure. But what happens if your journey is longer than it takes to eat a chocolate bar? You either drag the bar out, leaving gaps between each mouthful so that it lasts the journey, or you eat it in one go and spend the rest of the journey wishing you had another one.

You've probably seen people on the train or bus, trying to make their confectionery last. You may well have done it yourself. You take a bite, swallow it and quickly want the next bite, but you know you've got a long way to go so you hold yourself back. You deny yourself your next fix for several minutes. During this time you can't concentrate on anything else. All you can think about is that next mouthful of chocolate. When you finally allow yourself to have it the relief is so great that you devour the chocolate without pausing to taste it.

It's only a matter of time before you start buying more chocolate to last the whole journey, so you can avoid having to spend any of the time feeling deprived.

What you need to realize is that the restless feeling that you associate with your journey home is not helped by the chocolate bar; it's caused by it. Free yourself from your addiction to BAD SUGAR and you will approach the journey home in a much more relaxed state of mind. You'll find it a great deal easier to concentrate on other things, such as reading a book or newspaper, or even catching up with your work if you have to, and the journey will become an enjoyable and satisfying daily routine.

If you are hungry during your commute, there is an endless selection of readily available, easy-to-carry, easy-to-eat fruit at your disposal.

There is so much more to freedom from BAD SUGAR addiction than avoiding chocolate bars or puddings or cakes. Once you are free from BAD SUGAR, living without it is actually the most natural, easiest way of living you could imagine. Life becomes so much easier and more enjoyable.

All the so-called pleasures that you associate with BAD SUGAR are put in your mind by brainwashing and addiction. When you free yourself from the tyranny of the Big Monster and destroy the Little Monster, you will be amazed how much more enjoyable life becomes. You will feel more relaxed, more energetic, more at ease with yourself and healthier. In other words, **YOU HAVE NOTHING TO LOSE AND EVERYTHING TO GAIN.**

A NEW STATE OF MIND

From a very early age, before you were even old enough to understand, you have been brainwashed into believing that you love BAD SUGAR foods like cakes, biscuits, sweets, pasta, potato products and rice, but you have come to see that they don't love you. We're all aware of the harmful effects of BAD SUGAR even from a relatively early age. We associate it with being fat and having bad teeth. There is no illusion that BAD SUGAR is not harmful; now you need to go one step further and accept that BAD SUGAR provides absolutely no benefit whatsoever.

When you can see that, you will find the desire for sugary foods quickly goes and quitting becomes easy. Any thoughts you had that you would have to stop a runaway train are replaced with the joy of realizing you are free.

Opening your mind requires no more effort than merely recognizing that the brainwashing exists, accepting that you have been a victim of it and making a conscious decision to start seeing things as they really are. From now on, you will find yourself analysing everything you eat, especially processed food, and questioning whether you really want to put it in your body. You'll be surprised how natural this feels but it's logical that it should feel natural: you are getting back in touch with Nature's Guide.

EAT AS MUCH OF YOUR FAVOURITE FOODS AS YOU WANT, WHENEVER YOU WANT, AS OFTEN AS YOU WANT, AND BE THE EXACT WEIGHT YOU WANT TO BE, WITHOUT DIETING, SPECIAL EXERCISE, USING WILLPOWER OR FEELING DEPRIVED

When you first read this claim you probably thought it sounded too good to be true. If it worked, surely everyone would be doing it. The fact is millions of people around the world have followed this method and found that it works. The only reason not everybody is doing it is because they haven't found it yet, or they've been misled into following the willpower method by someone they regard as an expert.

But you have kept reading because you can see the logic and the truth in the method and you want to see it through. The next step is to make the commitment to do something about it. The next instruction is the most exciting of all:

ELEVENTH INSTRUCTION: GO FOR IT!

------------------------ **SUMMARY** -------------------

- You're not trying to change the food industry, just your own susceptibility to it.

- To reverse the brainwashing, first accept that you have been brainwashed.

- Take the time to see good and bad foods as they really are.

- You have nothing to lose and everything to gain.

- Go for it!

TAKING CONTROL

You have learned the principles that will enable you to free yourself from BAD SUGAR addiction. Now it's time to put those principles into action.

• You know that your inability to control your consumption of sugar was due to BAD SUGAR addiction. The addiction was the result of consumption and brainwashing, which started from birth and is only being properly addressed for the first time now.

• You know that quitting easily and permanently requires you to kill two monsters: the Little Monster in your body that cries out for its sugar fix and the Big Monster in your brain that makes you believe that sugar gives you some sort of pleasure or crutch.

• You know that the addiction is 1 per cent physical

and 99 per cent mental. The physical craving is almost imperceptible. It's the brainwashing that causes the panic. Killing the Little Monster that cries out for sugar is easy, but first you must destroy the Big Monster in your mind.

- You know that quitting does not require willpower. In fact, the willpower method makes it impossible to get completely free. You only need willpower if you have a conflict of wills, a tug-of-war between your fear of continuing to eat BAD SUGAR and your fear that you will feel deprived and miserable if you have to live without it. Remove the illusion of pleasure by understanding that BAD SUGAR consumption is not natural and that it provides you with no benefits whatsoever; then winning the tug-of-war is easy. There's simply nothing to battle.

- You know that, aside from animals whose diets we control or corrupt, humankind is the only species that suffers eating disorders, and eating-related conditions like obesity and diabetes, because we override our instincts with intellect. Instinct is the leading authority on what's good for you. In the wild, in spite of an inexhaustible abundance of free of charge food, animals simply don't become overweight.

- You know that there is nothing in your genetic make-up that makes you prone to addiction. You do not have an addictive personality. You only became addicted because you took an addictive substance. Even if you can't accept that you do not have an addictive personality, it doesn't matter. The addiction is actually easy to break so you'll find it easy to get free.

• You know that you were brainwashed for years without noticing. Reversing the brainwashing is easy. All you have to do is open your mind and see things as they really are.

• You know that you don't need substitutes. The substitute theory is flawed. Substitutes only make make it harder to quit and keep you hooked.

• You know that you have nothing to fear. When you cut BAD SUGAR out of your diet, you sacrifice nothing whatsoever and gain more than you would have thought possible. Without refined sugar, processed and starchy carbs you will feel more energetic and healthy, you will find it easier to relax and concentrate, and you will enjoy social occasions more. Most of all, you will no longer feel like a slave.

These are the principles that help addicts to find their way out of the maze to freedom. If there are any points you are unclear about, go back and re-read the relevant chapter. You have come a long way in a short space of time and you are on the brink of completing your escape. It is essential that you go out fully equipped with the mindset to succeed, and not like the prisoner who fears life on the outside.

In addition to the addiction principles, you have also learned how to apply Nature's Guide to help you eat both enjoyably and healthily.

- You know which foods really taste the best: fresh fruit, vegetables, nuts and seeds. You also know that these are the foods that are ideally suited to mankind. They can be eaten in their natural state and are the easiest for us to digest, and they yield all the nutrients that we need. These are our favourite foods.

- You know that the best way to satisfy hunger and to feel great is to eat raw, high-water-content food.

- You know to be wary of nuts and seeds with excess salt. Increasing your salt intake by eating them is likely to cause a problem, so avoid heavily salted nuts and seeds. Your restored sense of taste will appreciate your choice!

- You know which foods to avoid: processed foods, processed and starchy carbs, foods that you wouldn't eat raw and without the addition of sauces, fruit, vegetables, and seasoning as well as those that contain BAD SUGAR. Most secondary foods like meat and fish require cooking to make them edible and are not well suited to the human digestive system. They are not digested as efficiently, and leave more waste, which in some cases gets stored as fat. You do not have to avoid secondary foods entirely, but the more meals you eat without them, the better you'll feel and when you do include them in a meal don't make them the main feature. Reverse your thinking: when you do decide to eat them, have them as a small side with lots of fresh vegetables and salads.

• Refined sugar is an empty carb. It gives you calories, but no nutritional benefits whatsoever. It's the same with other processed carbohydrates like rice, pasta and bread. Potatoes are a starchy carb and cause a spike in blood sugar. All these items are BAD SUGAR foods and cause you a problem in the form of BAD SUGAR addiction.

TO JUICE OR NOT TO JUICE?

Of course, many people who drink juice and smoothies are incredibly healthy and athletic, but if you have a "BAD SUGAR problem", then juice and smoothies are potentially going to be a problem for you. Juicing or blending fruit alone creates a sugar bomb which the body can struggle to cope with. Juicing and blending is processing and it changes the balance of the fruit.

Within days of eliminating BAD SUGAR from your diet, just the thought of drinking processed, super-sweet fruit juice will cease to appeal. Your palate simply won't be tempted by it. Would you enjoy juicing vegetables with small quantities of fruit in order to limit your intake of sugar? Maybe. But what's the point?

Unfortunately, juicing eliminates fibre. When you eat a whole apple or orange, the sugar it contains is balanced by the fibre content, and digestion takes place at a natural pace, giving the liver a chance to fully metabolize it. Drinking half a pint of fruit juice, or smoothie, floods the digestive system with sugar in a way that eating fruit simply does not. Even fruit smoothies can cause an issue, because although the fibre is blended into the drink, it is effectively ripped to pieces and rendered ineffective. Fruit juice and fruit smoothies should be avoided. Drinking low sugar juice or smoothie recipes that mix small amounts of fruit with vegetables is probably less of a problem, but not the most natural way of enjoying your favourite food.

• The fact that in the 21st century, intelligent human beings have been convinced that they might need special "energy drinks" is testimony to the power of advertising and marketing. You don't need energy drinks and neither do your children, no matter how active they are. One of the saddest sights you are likely to see is kids picking up their cocktail of BAD SUGAR and caffeine, in the form of energy drinks, on the way to school. Red Bull or Monster for breakfast? It's not just ridiculous, it's dangerous and affects every aspect of the child's education and development. There are even reports of youngsters turning to cannabis to negate the effects of the pints of energy drink that they consume on a daily basis. What an extraordinary situation we've created by a simple lack of education. You know when to eat: when you're genuinely hungry. You understand about the false hunger created by an addictive craving for refined sugar, processed and starchy carbs. Eating is only a genuine pleasure when you're hungry. Overeating is eating when you're not hungry and gives no satisfaction.

- You know when to stop eating: when your hunger is satisfied. You understand the importance of eating slowly, to give your body time to register that it has received the nutrients it needs. You also understand that if you fill up on BAD SUGAR foods that don't provide the nutrients you need, you will never satisfy your hunger. When you eat your favourite foods, you get the nutrients you need and your fuel gauge tells you when you're satisfied. Heed it.

- You know that if you're trying to lose weight, there is no need to set yourself a target weight. Wild animals don't do this and they're never overweight. You'll know when you've achieved your ideal weight when you can look in the mirror and be happy with what you see.

- You know that dieting doesn't work because it leaves you feeling deprived. By following Easyway, you will achieve your ideal weight without feeling deprived or miserable, and you will enjoy every meal.

You have opened your mind to a lot of new thinking and any doubts you may have had when you started this book have been replaced with simple logic. You are ready for a wonderful life change.

WHAT TO EAT

When you quit smoking, it is essential that you quit completely. Cutting down doesn't work; it makes the problem worse. The only way to cure a nicotine addiction is to stop taking nicotine. With sugar addiction, the situation is more complicated. There is added sugar and processed and starchy carbs in so many foods that it would be virtually impossible to avoid the accidental consumption of small amounts of BAD SUGAR unless you exclusively eat only fruit and vegetables. I'm not advocating that, although you will find that your desire for secondary foods diminishes once you're free from the BAD SUGAR trap.

In Chapter 5, we explained how sugar gets you hooked by causing a spike in your blood sugar, which then leaves an empty feeling when it subsides. This is how the addiction takes hold. The foods to avoid, therefore, are the foods that cause this spike.

You can find out what these are by referring to the glycaemic index (GI). This is an index of all foods showing the amount by which they raise your blood sugar, and you can easily find it online. In tandem with the GI is another index, the glycaemic load (GL), which is calculated on the basis of the proportion of carbohydrate in the food and thereby gives a more accurate indication of the amount by which it will raise your blood sugar level. Watermelon, for example, has a high GI of 72 but a low GL of just 4.

As a guide, a GL of 0–10 is considered low, 11–19 medium and anything over 20 is high. The foods with the lowest GL are best. Most medium to high GL foods should be avoided. Included in this category are:

- Breakfast cereals
- White pasta
- White rice
- Bread
- Raisins
- Potatoes
- Fizzy drinks

All these foods will cause an abnormal rise in your blood sugar level and should be avoided.

Top of the list are foods packed with refined sugar:

- Cakes
- Biscuits
- Snack bars
- Sweets
- Desserts

In other words, all those so-called "goodies" that we are conditioned from birth to regard as our favourite foods. You now know that these are not your favourite foods. They don't even taste good. You only thought they did because you had been brainwashed into believing they were your favourite food and eating them temporarily satisfied the Little Monster, giving you the illusion of pleasure.

You don't have to poison yourself with these foods any more. Isn't that great? Unlike the addict who tries to quit with the willpower method, you won't feel deprived and miserable because you can't have these foods, you'll feel wonderful because you don't have to.

TWELFTH INSTRUCTION: GL IS ONLY A GUIDE. TO BE SURE THAT YOU ARE FREE FROM BAD SUGAR ADDICTION, CUT OUT REFINED SUGAR ITEMS, PROCESSED CARB ITEMS AND STARCHY CARB ITEMS (THIS INCLUDES PRETTY MUCH ALL READY-MADE MEALS AND PROCESSED FOODS)

If in the early days after you quit you feel the cries of the Little Monster, you no longer have to respond to those cries by eating BAD SUGAR. You don't have to respond at all. You can sit back, do nothing and enjoy the feeling. It isn't painful, it's barely perceptible, and it means the Little Monster is dying.

MUST I GIVE UP ALCOHOL TOO?

Firstly, you are not "giving up" anything. Easyway does not involve any sacrifice; on the contrary, you are only making wonderful gains. Alcoholic drinks are made with added sugar, though most of it turns to alcohol. Alcoholic drinks may not compound sugar addiction, but they will have a negative effect on your blood sugar in other ways.

People who consume an excessive amount of alcohol will find it can impair the effectiveness of insulin, resulting in high blood sugar levels. Even if you don't drink regularly, occasional bouts of heavy drinking can cause an insulin spike, resulting in low blood sugar. And drinking on an empty stomach, especially after exercise, can also hamper the body's ability to restore blood sugar to a healthy level.

If you want to lose weight and change body shape it is almost impossible to do so unless you reduce your intake of alcohol.

Wine, beers and cocktails all contain damaging amounts of sugar if consumed too often and/or in large amounts. So why not decide to take a break from alcohol for the first month or two of your new life? You're likely to feel amazing.

You shouldn't have a problem reducing your alcohol intake, mainly because you are going to be feeling, and looking, like a million dollars. However, in the event that you struggle you might want to read *Allen Carr's Easy Way to Control Alcohol* or *Allen Carr's Stop Drinking Now*, or you can attend one of our clinics, which are listed at the back of this book.

JUICES AND SMOOTHIES

Remember, one of the attributes of fruit is its fibre, which helps to slow down the rate at which the fructose (fruit sugar) is metabolized into the bloodstream. Juicing removes the fibre and blending a smoothie pulverizes the fibres to smithereens, leaving the sugar to pass very quickly into the bloodstream and cause a spike.

In addition to this, juicing and blending involves a larger quantity of fruit than you would normally consume if eating the whole fruit. Most people eat one orange or sometimes two in one go. It takes around **13–15 oranges** to produce 1 litre of juice. That means that a normal-sized glass of juice contains four to five oranges, which means you're putting two to four times the amount of fructose into your body than you normally would. That coupled with the lack of fibre can have a severe effect on your blood sugar levels. As mentioned, there are many healthy, athletic people who drink juice and smoothies, but if you have a BAD SUGAR problem, this should be avoided.

BEWARE OF DRIED FRUIT

Dried fruit has the water removed and therefore concentrates the sugar. There's a huge difference between eating a couple of fresh apricots versus eating a couple of dried ones. Firstly, who only eats a couple of dried ones? Most people end up eating a bagful. If dried apricots were equal in sugar that would be bad enough, but in fact dried apricots contain 12 times more sugar than fresh apricots. It's not just the sugar that is concentrated, it's the fibre as well. Stripped of water, the fruit becomes harder to digest. In short, it's another processed food and the sweetness is transformed by the processing it undergoes. Your taste buds will change so much once you escape from BAD SUGAR that you won't really seek out that level of sweetness any more.

There are plenty of healthy people who eat dried fruit but if you have a BAD SUGAR problem you should avoid it.

THE BEST WAY TO GET COOL, REFRESHING, NUTRITIOUS FRUIT JUICE IS BY EATING FRUIT

And, it goes without saying, avoid artificial fruit juices; they're packed with sugar too.

THE MARGIN FOR ERROR

The human body is an incredible machine. Unlike your car, you can put the wrong fuel into it and it will not immediately grind to a halt. As long as you follow your instincts and make your favourite foods, as designated by Nature's Guide, the cornerstone of your diet, you can continue to eat a wide range of secondary foods, if you want to. You will find, though, that your desire for them diminishes as you become more and more attuned to your instincts.

Our aim is to free you from your addiction to BAD SUGAR. The important thing is that you avoid the foods that cause a sugar spike. Do this and you will quickly kill the Little Monster.

If you do happen to eat or drink something containing BAD SUGAR by mistake or if you have a crazy moment when your judgement was impaired, don't panic. This doesn't mean you're still hooked, or that you are going to get hooked again. The only way you can get hooked is by allowing the Big Monster back into your mind.

The Little Monster may be temporarily reawakened, but you have killed the Big Monster, so all you have to do is brush yourself off, remind yourself that you get no pleasure or crutch from the sugar and enjoy the feeling of freedom you get from knowing that you no longer have to eat or drink it again.

This is one of the ways in which BAD SUGAR addiction varies from, for example, nicotine addiction. One puff of a cigarette and a former smoker eventually reverts to smoking. With sugar, because of the way the body copes with natural sugars, there is a margin for error. Having said that, take care not to abuse it. It's like a seatbelt in a car; the idea isn't to repeatedly make use of its lifesaving function by driving erratically, it's there in the event of an accident.

YOUR EATING ROUTINE

We have stated that you should only eat when hungry. You may be thinking that this sounds impractical. Most people eat three meals a day: one in the morning, one in the middle of the day and one in the evening. It's a routine that fits around the working day and it's not very flexible. So how can you adapt this routine so that you only eat when hungry?

In fact, you don't have to adapt the routine at all, because it already corresponds to the natural cycle of your digestive system. The typical working day was designed to fit around eating, not the other way round. That's why with traditional working patterns work stops for lunch and finishes in time for the evening meal. This routine allows your hunger to build up between meals and so it also allows you to enjoy each meal to the full.

In addition, hunger is very flexible. Most of the time we're not even aware of it. Even when we are, it is easy to live with the feeling until such time arises when it is convenient for us to eat. If you are occupied with work or recreation, you won't notice that you're hungry. If your attention is drawn to it, by a smell of food, say, there is still no problem. You don't suffer. On the contrary, you can enjoy letting your hunger build, knowing that the longer it goes on, the better the food will taste when you do get round to eating. This ability to sustain hunger, usually without even realizing it, gives you the flexibility to eat at such times as satisfy both your hunger and your lifestyle.

HUNGER IS NOT TO BE FEARED

Satisfying hunger is a great pleasure and, provided you follow Nature's Guide, it's one you can enjoy every day for the rest of your life.

What's important is that you make the timing, volume and substance of your meals suit your own selfish needs. If you don't feel hungry at lunchtime, don't feel obliged to eat. The routine of three meals a day is perfectly suited to eating healthily and enjoyably, but it doesn't suit everyone. The golden rule is to heed your natural fuel gauge and eat only when hungry. Everybody's fuel gauge is different and it's essential that you are in tune with your own.

Three meals a day works for most people because it allows enough time for hunger to build up, but only provided you don't graze between meals. People who pick at food all day tend to believe that it is something in their nature that makes them that way like a grazing animal. But human beings were not designed to graze. Chimpanzees don't graze; sheep do. We have much more in common with the former. The reason people feel the need to constantly pick at food is because they are permanently hungry and that's because they are eating the wrong types of foods, which don't satisfy the body's demand for nutrients.

Start eating the foods that were designed for you and you will find that the desire to keep grazing soon disappears.

SUMMARY

- You have all the knowledge you need to quit easily and permanently.

- Cut out refined sugar items, processed carb items, and starchy carb items (this includes pretty much all ready-made meals and processed foods).

- Alcohol can affect your blood sugar levels and can stop you being the shape that you want to be.

- The best way to get fruit juice is by eating fruit.

- If you ever make a mistake, don't panic.

- Make the timing, volume and substance of your meals suit your own selfish needs.

WITHDRAWAL

When you quit using Easyway, any sensation of withdrawal becomes a source of pleasure.

Soon you are going to consume your final BAD SUGAR meal and make a solemn vow never to consume it again. First, though, there is one final aspect of addiction that we need to address: withdrawal.

The cycle of addiction involves the creation of an empty, insecure feeling, caused by a drug leaving your body that appears to be relieved with the appearance of a "high" or "boost" when the drug is taken again.

At this point in proceedings, you may be concerned that the withdrawal will pose a stern physical challenge to your attempt to quit BAD SUGAR.

There are two things you should know about withdrawal:

1. You already know what it feels like. You have experienced

it after every occasion you've consumed BAD SUGAR every single day of your life.

2. Even nicotine addicts only find it physically gruelling if they believe they are being deprived and that they are sacrificing something.

Whenever you eat or drink BAD SUGAR (which for you is probably at least six times a day – most likely a lot more) it causes a spike in blood sugar, followed by a low as your body adjusts. This low is accompanied by a slightly restless, mildly anxious or fatigued feeling: the Little Monster crying out for more BAD SUGAR. This feeling is so slight as to be almost imperceptible. This is the sensation described as withdrawal.

Often the fear of physical withdrawal symptoms is enough to prevent a lot of addicts from even trying to quit, but, as with most addictions, it's the psychological dependence that needs the most work rather than the physical dependence – and with Easyway, you've already mastered that.

THE SYMPTOMS

You may have read about the symptoms of withdrawal:
- Extreme anxiety
- Irritability
- Mood swings
- Extreme nervousness
- Depression

• Confusion

Although these manifest themselves physically – they have no physical cause – the cause is psychological. And they are symptoms that every addict suffers to a greater or lesser degree WHILE THEY ARE HOOKED. The only unpleasant symptoms are caused by the mental process of feeling deprived. The addict experiences a mild discomfort triggered by the withdrawal feeling (the Little Monster), and that triggers a feeling of deprivation, a strong yearning, entirely caused by the mental process "I WANT IT – I CAN'T HAVE IT – AGHHHH!"

Like a tantrum, this thought process, rather than the physical withdrawal, causes the really unpleasant symptoms.

If you understand that you get nothing from BAD SUGAR, no pleasure, no enjoyment, no benefit, then you won't want it. If you don't want it you simply won't have that "AGHHHHHHH" feeling.

Some people do suffer mild symptoms when they come off BAD SUGAR: a headache, slightly restless, mildly anxious, or a fatigued feeling, but they are incredibly mild as long as they don't cause you to panic.

In fact, you probably won't even notice them at all. If you do have a headache, take an aspirin (making sure of course that it is sugar free).

All in all, those mild symptoms, even if you notice them, are worth living with for a couple of days in return for freedom and **A BRAND NEW YOU.**

Be quite clear that BAD SUGAR causes these feelings; it doesn't relieve them. When you understand that, you don't feel any sense of deprivation and the physical symptoms disappear.

IF YOU CONTINUE TO CONSUME BAD SUGAR, YOU'LL SUFFER THAT EMPTY, INSECURE FEELING FOR THE REST OF YOUR LIFE

As long as you realize that the slightly empty, insecure feeling is caused by the last BAD SUGAR you consumed, and that the one thing that will ensure you suffer that feeling for the rest of your life will be to consume more, you will find it easy and painless to quit.

Countless smokers who have tried and failed to quit with the willpower method because they couldn't withstand the agony of withdrawal have been amazed at how easily they've been able to quit with Easyway. They've endured none of the suffering that they had gone through in previous attempts because they no longer believed they were being deprived. On the contrary, they experienced a wonderful feeling of freedom.

Exactly the same applies to you and BAD SUGAR. When you realize that any pleasure or crutch is just an illusion, you feel no sense of deprivation and, consequently, no misery or torture. Just a wonderful feeling of freedom.

ENJOYING WITHDRAWAL

When you quit BAD SUGAR for good, you might experience that mild craving for a few days. Remind yourself that this is not a physical pain; it's just the faint cries of the Little Monster wanting to be fed. Be conscious of the feeling and delight in it.

The Little Monster was created when you first started consuming BAD SUGAR and it has continued to feed on every piece of BAD SUGAR food or drink you've had since. As soon as you stop consuming BAD SUGAR, you cut off the supply and that evil monster begins to die.

In its death throes, it will try to entice you to feed it. Create a mental image of this parasite getting weaker and weaker and enjoy starving it to death.

Enjoy the death throes of the Little Monster because you will by now understand the cause and know that the monster inside you is dying.

Even if you have thoughts of eating or drinking BAD SUGAR for a few days, don't worry about it. It takes time to adjust to any change. This is true of all changes like a new house or a new car. At those moments, just remind yourself how lucky you are to be free. That will be easy because…

YOU WILL FEEL LIKE A MILLION DOLLARS!

IMPORTANT ADVICE FOR THOSE WITH TYPE 2 DIABETES CONTROLLED BY MEDICATION, OR THOSE WHO TAKE BLOOD PRESSURE MEDICATION OR ANY OTHER MEDICATION THAT COULD BE AFFECTED BY DIET AND/OR DRAMATIC WEIGHT LOSS:

If you are on medication, talk to your GP. This is particularly important because he or she should be involved in monitoring and adjusting your medicines. You may need to be firm with your doctor. The chances are they may be resistant to your plan to cure your condition by adjusting your diet. More and more doctors are discovering that this is not only possible, but incredibly easy. However, many remain resistant. Explain to them what you intend to do and ask them to support you and recommend how you should monitor and adjust your medication based on your plan.

WHEN CAN I SAY I'M CURED?

The good news is that with Easyway you can start enjoying the genuine pleasure of being free from BAD SUGAR addiction from the moment you finish your final BAD SUGAR meal. Unlike the willpower method, you don't have to wait to be free, waiting for something to *not* happen.

It takes just a few days for the feeling of physical withdrawal to pass. During this time, people who use the willpower method tend to feel completely obsessed with being denied what they see as their pleasure or support. Then, after about three weeks, there comes a moment when they suddenly realize that they have not thought about BAD SUGAR for a while. It's an exciting feeling... and a dangerous moment.

They've gone from believing that life will always be miserable without sugar to believing that time will solve their problem. They feel great and believe that surely this is the cure. It's time to celebrate. What possible harm could it do to reward themselves with just a little sugar?

It's clear that the Big Monster is still alive. They still believe that they have been denying themselves some sort of pleasure. If they are stupid enough to give in to this belief and eat BAD SUGAR, they won't find it rewarding at all. It will give them no feeling of pleasure or crutch. The only reason they ever experienced the illusion of pleasure was that it partially relieved the feelings of withdrawal.

But that one shot of BAD SUGAR is enough to revive the Little Monster. Now panic starts to creep back in. They don't want their efforts to quit to be blown away so easily and for nothing, so they draw on all their willpower and make sure they don't respond to the urge to have BAD SUGAR again.

But after a while the same thing happens. They regain their confidence and the temptation to have "just a little" rears its ugly head again. This time they can say to themselves, "I did it last time and didn't get hooked, so what's the harm in doing it again?" They're just wandering back into the trap.

Does this ring any bells? Anyone who has tried to quit with the willpower method is likely to have experienced this scenario. With Easyway, when you realize you haven't thought about BAD SUGAR for a while, your first thought is not to celebrate with BAD SUGAR food or drink; it's **YIPPEE! I'M FREE!**

There is no feeling of deprivation. You can relax from the

moment you finish your final BAD SUGAR meal, provided you fully understand that any mild feelings you have are harmless physical withdrawal, and any thoughts of eating or drinking BAD SUGAR are simply caused by years of brainwashing. Rather than thinking, "I want some and can't have some" or "I wish I could have it" you think, "Yes! Isn't it marvellous! I'm free."

Addicts who quit with the willpower method never get to the point where they can say that with certainty. They are never quite sure when they've kicked it. They are waiting for the desire to go, hoping that they'll wake up one day and not want it any more.

Those who rely on willpower set themselves a goal: never to have BAD SUGAR for the rest of their lives. But how do they know when they've achieved that goal? They have to wait the rest of their lives. No wonder they never feel free.

But if you know that you've escaped from a terrible trap, one that damaged and threatened the length, quality and enjoyment of your future life, one that stole your energy, your self-esteem, your fitness, your vitality, one that made you feel guilty, ashamed and embarrassed – if you escape that, when would you start to rejoice?

RIGHT NOW! Don't wait for a few days or a week or a month. Rejoice at your freedom from the moment you become free. That is the moment you decide never to have BAD SUGAR again.

THE MOMENT HAS ARRIVED

Soon you'll have your final BAD SUGAR meal and make a solemn vow never to consume BAD SUGAR again. If this thought makes you panic, remind yourself of these simple facts:

- The food industry depends on that panic to keep you hooked. It creates that panic and manipulates it with advertising, marketing, and the addictive ingredients it puts in its "food".

- BAD SUGAR doesn't relieve the panic; it causes it.

If you have already stopped eating and drinking BAD SUGAR, please don't worry. You don't need to have the ritual of the last BAD SUGAR meal. At this point just confirm that you have already had it and follow the remaining instructions.

Either way, take a moment to collect your thoughts and compose yourself. Do you really have any reason to panic? Nothing bad is going to happen as a result of you cutting out BAD SUGAR. You have only marvellous gains to make.

Perhaps you're afraid of going into unknown territory, like the long-term prisoner being released. There is nothing unfamiliar about what you are about to do. It is something you have already done tens of thousands of times before, every time you've finished your last meal or snack containing BAD SUGAR.

This particular BAD SUGAR meal will be a very, very special one. It will be your last.

You are achieving something marvellous and in a matter of days you will start to reap the benefits. You will feel stronger, both physically and mentally. You will have more energy, more confidence, more self-respect and even more money. It is vital that you don't delay this wonderful freedom, not for a week, or a day. Waiting is one of the reasons why addicts using the willpower method find it so difficult. They put off the "evil day", hoping that the problem will go away by itself.

You become a "non-BAD SUGAR addict" the moment you finish your final BAD SUGAR meal. You have a new frame of mind, an understanding that BAD SUGAR, refined sugar, processed carbs and starchy carbs do nothing for you and that by not consuming BAD SUGAR you are freeing yourself from a life of slavery, misery and degradation. Replace any panic you may have felt with a feeling of excitement. You no longer need to suffer. You're about to discover the joy of taking control and finding every meal a genuine pleasure. Rejoice! This is going to be one of the best experiences of your life. And it just keeps going on, and on, and on.

You're achieving wonderful positive gains, not least the changes in your moods that you'll notice almost immediately. You'll be amazed by the simple absence of mood swings which you may have previously believed to be part of everyday life. They were caused by the constant intense fluctuations in your blood sugars.

In a few days you will start to notice the change in your body shape and observe how those changes increase as weeks fly by. The thought of those foods that you used to crave, rather than fill you with desire, will leave you feeling cold and unmoved.

I've talked about meat and fish earlier in this book. By all means have them occasionally but in small amounts. Have them in portions dwarfed by the amazing, nutritious, fresh salad and vegetables that will be among your new favourite foods.

You can get free of BAD SUGAR while carrying on drinking alcohol (as prescribed on pages 209 and 210), but if you really want to see a dramatic change in your body shape and weight, reduce your alcohol intake to an absolute minimum. You're not reading this book in order to quit drinking, so unless you want to do so, you don't need to. Just be aware that if you want to change body shape and lose weight then you need to dramatically reduce your intake of alcohol. As mentioned in Chapter 16, if you have any problem with that in the future, or if your alcohol intake causes you concern, then by all means read *Allen Carr's Easy Way to Control Alcohol* or *Allen Carr's Stop Drinking Now.*

Likewise with cheese and dairy products, you don't need to reduce your intake of those foods to be free of BAD SUGAR addiction. But if you want to dramatically change your body shape and weight, then you need to control your intake. A litte feta cheese in your salad at lunchtime or in the evening won't cause you a problem. Neither will milk in your tea. But remember, a lot of the cheese and dairy products that you've consumed has been to make BAD SUGAR products palatable. If you don't eat much bread, you don't tend to eat much butter and cheese. Likewise with pasta and pizza. If you don't eat cereal, your consumption of milk is dramatically reduced.

So be careful with those foods if you want to change your body shape and weight and you will succeed. In fact, I should warn you: your body will change extraordinarily quickly if you reduce them to a minimum. If you take this option, then your life will change even more dramatically than merely escaping from BAD SUGAR addiction. You'll be almost unrecognizable.

YOU ARE ABOUT TO BE FREE!

SUMMARY

- Recognize any feelings of withdrawal as the death throes of the Little Monster and enjoy them.

- Addicts suffer withdrawal pangs all the time. Non-addicts don't suffer them at all. You're going to be a non-addict.

- Get into a positive frame of mind: feel the excitement of what you are achieving.

Chapter 18

YOUR FINAL BAD SUGAR MEAL

IN THIS CHAPTER
•PICKING YOUR MOMENT
•LAST-MINUTE NERVES •THE RITUAL
•NEVER MIND THE OUTCOME

The ritual of the final BAD SUGAR meal is where you break the cycle of addiction and get free. Unless you've already stopped consuming BAD SUGAR, it's important that you observe the ritual and then get on with enjoying life.

You've reached the point that every addict dreams of: the moment when you escape the trap and begin life as a non-addict. Your slavery to BAD SUGAR is about to become a thing of the past. All through the book I've assured you that escape would be easy, but that shouldn't lessen your sense of achievement in any way. To go through the method as instructed, in order to understand your own nature and the nature of the trap, requires discipline and perseverance. It also takes courage to open your mind. So be proud of your achievement. You've reached a position that more and more BAD SUGAR addicts are wishing they could achieve. You may be wondering when to pick your moment.

MEANINGLESS DAYS

When addicts make an attempt to quit with the willpower method, they tend to pick a time that feels significant, thinking that the occasion will help to strengthen their resolve. These occasions fall into two categories: traumatic events, such as a health scare, and landmark days, such as the old favourite, New Year's Day. These days are meaningless. They have no bearing on your addiction; in fact, they cause more harm than good. New Year is a time for resolutions. We make a decision to apply our willpower to make a change in our lives for the better. This is usually because we have overindulged so horribly on junk over the Christmas period that we feel genuinely sick with ourselves. What better time to change our ways?

In fact, there couldn't be a worse time. A few days into January your self-loathing has disappeared and you've forgotten how grim your old way of eating made you feel. You only tried to change through force of will and now that your resolve has weakened you see no reason for depriving yourself any more. The illusion that BAD SUGAR foods give you some sort of pleasure or a crutch remains steadfastly intact and you remain just as hooked as ever.

New Year's Day is the worst example, but all meaningless days are harmful in the same way. All they do is provide an excuse for avoiding the most obvious solution for every addict:

STOP NOW!

If you've had a health scare, please don't attempt to make that your motivation; just use your improved health as a wonderful bonus to enjoy when you are free. There is no better time to stop than right now. You have read and understood all the instructions and, like a boxer about to go into the ring, you are in peak condition. You have nothing to fear and only marvellous gains to make, so why wait? Today is the most significant day of your life: it is the day you break free.

FEELING NERVOUS?

It's normal to feel some nerves at this stage. Don't worry about that. Nerves are a sign of your excitement at the power you now hold in your hands and they are no threat whatsoever to your chances of success. Every great sportsperson has butterflies in their stomach before their big event, but as they warm up and prepare themselves mentally they cast their minds back to their training and quickly see the benefits, their confidence grows and they begin to enjoy the anticipation of the contest ahead. They survey their competitors who by comparison look weak and ill-prepared.

Words cannot do justice to the utter joy you feel when you finally accept you don't need to consume BAD SUGAR any more. The elation is unbelievable. It's like a huge, dark shadow lifting from your mind. You no longer need to despise yourself, or have to worry about what it's been doing to your health, or all the money you've wasted. You no longer have to worry about junk food anymore. You no longer feel weak, miserable, sordid, incomplete or guilty.

You have all the knowledge and understanding you need to make this the best experience of your life. Soon you will be beating your mortal enemy. Rejoice in that prospect. Be merciless.

You have nothing to fear. Remind yourself that you are not "giving up" anything. All those empty carbs give you nothing but ill health, guilt and misery. If you've followed and understood everything up to this point, you'll have come to the obvious conclusion: **THERE IS NO REASON TO CONSUME BAD SUGAR.**

Very soon I'll ask you to eat your final BAD SUGAR meal and make a solemn vow that you will never consume BAD SUGAR again. It's essential that you are completely reconciled with that notion. You must be absolutely clear that BAD SUGAR gives you no pleasure or crutch whatsoever and that you are not making any sort of sacrifice.

If you find the thought of never having another plate of pasta or chips, or another cake, biscuit, chocolate, or sweet difficult to fully accept, try taking on board the only alternative: spending the rest of your life never being free. Never being allowed to stop.

It's a simple choice: freedom or slavery. It's incredibly easy to stop consuming BAD SUGAR provided you follow all the instructions. Your main reason for stopping is because you hate feeling like a slave, so instead of thinking, "I must never eat *BAD SUGAR* again," start thinking, "This is great! I don't ever need to have that again. I don't ever need to feel stuffed and unhealthy and guilty and miserable after I've eaten again. I'M FREE!"

THE INSTRUCTIONS

If you have any doubts in your mind about what you are about to do, please go back and re-read the relevant chapters, keeping an open mind and questioning everything that you have been told about BAD SUGAR in your life.

THE RITUAL

If you are absolutely clear and happy about everything you've learned, you will no doubt be champing at the bit to get on with your escape. The only doubt you may have is whether you actually want to bother with the ritual of the final BAD SUGAR meal.

Some people have what they hope will be their last BAD SUGAR before they begin this book and by the time they reach this stage they are adamant that they have no desire ever to eat BAD SUGAR again. If this applies to you, that's great news because it means you have completely removed the desire for BAD SUGAR. There is no need to go back on that, but it is still important that you go through the ritual of making your vow.

While smokers, drinkers and other drug addicts can usually remember a time in their life before they became hooked, this is not true of BAD SUGAR addicts. The slavery begins at a young age. So this is a momentous occasion in your life and one of the most important decisions you will ever make. You are freeing yourself from slavery and achieving something amazing, something all BAD SUGAR addicts would love to achieve and something that everybody, addicts and non-addicts alike, will admire you for.

Most importantly, you will soar in the estimations of one person in particular: yourself.

That's an achievement that deserves to be marked with some ceremony. The ritual of the final BAD SUGAR meal will give you something positive to look back on should the memory of how good you feel now begin to fade.

The most important purpose of the ritual, though, is this: it marks a moment in time, the end point of your addiction. With the willpower method, the thing that makes it difficult to quit is the waiting and the doubt that creeps in as you wait for time to cure your problem. With this method, you become a non-addict the moment you finish your BAD SUGAR meal and make your vow to become free from addiction to BAD SUGAR. It's important to know when that moment is, to be able to make that vow with a feeling of triumph, to visualize your victory over the Little Monster and be able to say, "Yes! I'm no longer an addict. I'm FREE!"

Your mind should be absolutely made up. It is not enough to *hope* that you will never eat BAD SUGAR again, you need to be 100 per cent certain. So let's strike one final blow against the ideas that may cause you to doubt your decision to quit:

1. Remove the belief that you are making a sacrifice.

Get it clearly into your mind that there is absolutely nothing to give up. BAD SUGAR gives no genuine pleasure or crutch whatsoever. The fact that it appears to is just a subtle illusion caused by the cycle of addiction and brainwashing.

2. Remove the belief that it's possible to have the occasional splurge on BAD SUGAR without getting hooked again.

Remember there is only one way to stay free from BAD SUGAR and that is *not* to consume BAD SUGAR.

The one essential in order to be a "non-BAD SUGAR addict" for life is *never* to consume BAD SUGAR. In order to be *happy* to be free, you must never *desire* BAD SUGAR.

Over the next few days, weeks and months you're going to feel like a million dollars. You'll begin to notice dramatic changes in how you look and how you feel. If one night you make a mistake and find you've eaten or drunk something containing BAD SUGAR, don't panic!

Put it behind you. Your body can cope with an occasional blip, but your mind will not. Another dose of BAD SUGAR will revive the Big Monster. So just reconfirm to yourself how happy you are to be free and remain happily free of BAD SUGAR *from that moment on.*

Now make sure you are clear on these three additional ideas:

1. Remove the belief that you are a confirmed BAD SUGAR addict, or have an addictive personality, or are in some way different from all other people.

The characteristics that are common to addicts are caused by the addiction, they do not cause it. Anyone can fall for the BAD SUGAR trap, and most people do.

2. Avoid the influence of other BAD SUGAR addicts.

They're the ones who are losing out, not you. You now have much more expertise on the subject than they have. Pity them for their ignorance and feel compassion for them. In time, as they see how you change, they will envy your freedom and show interest in how you achieved it.

3. Avoid believing bad advice.

Some people will fail for this reason and, like the others who have, they will feel miserable. Please don't let it be you. It's hard to imagine how a nutritionist could possibly recommend that processed or starchy carbs should be the cornerstone of a healthy nutritious diet. Times are changing. As more nutritionists and doctors see the evidence of how BAD SUGAR addicts have turned their lives around; how Type 2 diabetes has been completely reversed in hundreds of thousands of cases, merely by cutting out BAD SUGAR and how its victims have become free from a lifetime of medication and health worries, the truth about BAD SUGAR and the havoc it has unleashed on the world will be fully exposed.

Before you read this book, you had some favourite foods that you thought you could never live without. It may have been pasta, bread, potato, chips, cake, biscuits, chocolate bars, puddings or sweets... or all of the above. Whatever it was, this is what you are going to eat as your final BAD SUGAR meal.

If you stopped eating sugar before you started the book, you can skip to the vow. If not, prepare your final BAD SUGAR meal as you used to do and start eating it. Whether it's just a small token sweet, or a three-course meal, prepare for it as you always have (bearing in mind the guidance you receive from your doctor if you are on medication). Before you take a bite of each item, focus on how it looks, how it smells and how it feels to the touch. See how unnatural it is.

Now take a bite. Pay attention to how it feels in your mouth. Don't swallow it immediately, but keep it in your mouth and think about the ingredients that make it up. What does it taste like? Is there any flavour? Is that perhaps the flavour of fruit? Is that the flavour of the accompanying sauce made of fruit or vegetables? What is making it edible? Is the flavour from secondary foods? Sense how it makes you feel as you swallow it. Sense how it feels as it makes its way through your body. You may even find it repulsive. Remember you're not giving up anything. You wouldn't eat a bowl of pasta without adding fat, cheese, meat, fish or vegetables. Remember, it's only BAD SUGAR that you're getting rid of. All the other flavours and tastes, the REAL flavours and REAL tastes will remain part of your life. It's only the junk, the starchy carbs and the refined sugar that you're escaping from.

As you eat, remind yourself of all you know about BAD SUGAR.

- It gives you no genuine pleasure or crutch.

- It doesn't relieve stress and anxiety; it causes it.

- The only reason you ever thought you needed it was because you ate BAD SUGAR in the first place.

THE VOW

Think about the misery and suffering that BAD SUGAR has caused you. Visualize the Little Monster and how it has wound you round its little finger for all these years. Imagine it laughing at you. This is the time for your revenge. You are going to knock that Little Monster clean out of the ring. As you swallow your last mouthful, make a vow never to eat BAD SUGAR again. Ever! No more slavery. No more misery. You are cutting off the Little Monster's lifeline and destroying that evil tyrant once and for all.

CONGRATULATIONS! YOU'VE WON!

Take delight in your victory. This is one of the greatest achievements of your life, if not the greatest. It's important that this moment sticks in your mind.

EXPECT THE UNEXPECTED

It's a wonderful facet of the human mind that if you're prepared for a challenge, it doesn't faze you as it would if it took you by surprise. You can easily guard against any moments of doubt in future simply by knowing that they will arise.

Right now, you are fired up with powerful reasons to stop consuming **BAD SUGAR,** but after a few weeks of freedom your memory of how miserable **BAD SUGAR** made you feel will dim. Fix those thoughts in your mind now while they are still vivid, so that even if your memory of the details should diminish, your resolution never to eat **BAD SUGAR** does not.

In a few months' time, you'll find it difficult to believe that you once found it necessary to eat **BAD SUGAR**, let alone how much it controlled your life, and consequently your fear of getting hooked again may dwindle. Be aware now, in advance, that this will be a danger period.

You might have moments when you're on a high, surrounded by other people eating cakes or biscuits, say, or you might suffer a trauma and your guard will be down. Anticipate these situations now and make it part of your vow so that, if and when they come, you will be prepared and not fooled into eating **BAD SUGAR**.

DON'T WAIT FOR THE OUTCOME

In the cycle of addiction, each fix creates the need or desire for the next. The moment you finish your last mouthful and make your vow, you break the cycle. You have put down a marker. This is the moment when you walk free.

You have nothing to wait for. You're ready to move on. Embrace this moment with a feeling of excitement and elation and start enjoying life free from BAD SUGAR. The nightmare is over.

FREEDOM STARTS HERE!

SUMMARY

• Don't worry about last-minute nerves; they're completely normal.

• The vow marks the moment when you become free. Make it and rejoice in it.

• You're free as soon as you make your vow. There is nothing to wait for.

• Anticipate dangerous situations and prepare your mindset in advance.

Chapter 19

ENJOYING LIFE
FREE FROM BAD SUGAR

IN THIS CHAPTER
• THE FIRST FEW DAYS
• COPING WITH DOWN DAYS • A USEFUL TIP
• YOUR FAVOURITE FOODS FOR LIFE

Congratulations! You've done it! You have freed yourself from addiction to BAD SUGAR and will remain free for life, provided you never doubt your decision to quit.

The aim of this book was to show you a way to free yourself from slavery to BAD SUGAR, rediscover the joy of eating and achieve a level of happiness and wellbeing that you didn't realize was possible. As a result of what you have achieved, you will find mealtimes more enjoyable, you will feel better about yourself now that you are able to control your eating and you will become fitter, be happy with your appearance and enjoy greater confidence.

In addition, you will be better equipped to handle stress, you will derive more pleasure from social occasions and you will feel more energetic. These are not benefits that lie in some faraway fantasy world; they are benefits you start to feel the moment you finish your final BAD SUGAR meal and make your vow to become free.

THE DEATH THROES

In the first few days after you finish your final BAD SUGAR meal, you may be aware of the Little Monster crying for BAD SUGAR. Don't ignore it. This is nothing to worry about. On the contrary, it's a sign that the Little Monster is dying. Recognize the cries and rejoice in what they signify: the monster that has held you in its power for all this time will soon be dead.

When you were a BAD SUGAR addict, the cries of the Little Monster had you hunting around for BAD SUGAR. It had you stuff huge quantities of junk, empty carbs, and other processed foods that were difficult to digest into your body. The monster had you wrapped around its little finger. Now you can just stand by and rejoice in its death. Picture a Little Monster searching around the desert for a drink and you having control of the water supply. All you have to do is keep it turned off. It's as easy as that. The method for killing the Little Monster couldn't be simpler:

DO NOTHING!

Many people don't even notice the death throes of the Little Monster; they're too busy enjoying life without being a slave to BAD SUGAR. Even at their worst, the death throes are no more uncomfortable than a slight empty insecure feeling, which only lasts for a few days. They only become a problem if you start to worry about them or interpret them as a need or desire for BAD SUGAR.

There is no need to try *not* to think about BAD SUGAR. You are free from that tyrant now; you can think about it as much as you like, as long as you never desire it. In fact, trying *not* to think about something is a sure way of becoming obsessed with it. Say you were told not to think of elephants: what's the first thing that pops into your mind?

You can think about BAD SUGAR and you can recognize the cries of the Little Monster, but prepare your mindset in advance so that you are ready with the right response. Instead of thinking, "I want it but I'm not allowed it," think, "This is the Little Monster demanding its fix. This is what I've been suffering throughout my life. Now I don't have to suffer any more. Isn't it great! I'm free and no longer an addict and so I'll soon be free of this feeling forever."

Be aware of the complete absence of physical pain and that the only discomfort you might be feeling is not because you've stopped eating BAD SUGAR but because you started in the first place. Also be clear that having more BAD SUGAR, far from relieving that discomfort, would ensure that you suffered it for the rest of your life.

SEEKING COMFORT

We all have our off days and there will be days when you find it hard to see the joy in life. This has nothing to do with the fact that you've quit BAD SUGAR and BAD SUGAR will not lighten your mood. What you will find is that when you're not addicted to BAD SUGAR the bad days don't come around so often, and when they do you feel stronger to cope with them.

You might well be confused and concerned to find that when you have a bad day, the thought of BAD SUGAR enters your mind. Don't worry, this is perfectly normal and you just have to recognize the thought for what it is: a remnant from the days when you responded to every setback by eating BAD SUGAR. It does not mean you're still hooked, or even vulnerable to getting hooked again. It just means you're still adjusting to your newfound freedom. Be prepared for these moments and respond not by thinking, "I mustn't eat BAD SUGAR," or, "I thought I'd overcome this addiction," but by telling yourself, "Great! I don't have to eat BAD SUGAR any more. I'm free!" These become moments of real pleasure rather than moments of concern or worry.

It is essential that you never doubt or question your decision to cut out BAD SUGAR. Never make the mistake that people on the willpower method make, of craving just one fix. If you do you will put yourself in the same impossible position as them: miserable if you don't have it, and even more miserable if you do.

LIFE STARTS HERE

One of the great benefits of curing your addiction to BAD SUGAR is that you rediscover the joy of life's genuine pleasures: all addicts lose the ability to enjoy the things that non-addicts enjoy most: reading books, getting out and about, watching entertainment, social occasions, exercise, sex... Their obsession with whatever they're addicted to makes everything else pale into insignificance and they become cynical and narrow-minded. Now that you've quit BAD SUGAR, you can start to embrace a whole world of REAL pleasures.

You will find that situations you have come to regard as unstimulating or even irritating become enjoyable again: things like spending time with your loved ones, going for walks, seeing friends. Work will become more enjoyable and you'll become better at what you do. When your mind is free from addiction you find it easier to concentrate, think creatively and to cope with pressure. Eating fresh, nutritious food is not just good for your body – it's wonderful for your brain and spirit too.

You also become more discerning and assertive about the things you *don't* like. Be fussy about what you eat. Take pleasure in feeding your body the correct fuel for life. When you're free from BAD SUGAR and you know the sort of food that makes you happy, it becomes easy to see the value, or lack of it, in junk eating and spare yourself unnecessary suffering. You will have the confidence to follow the path you know is best for you.

Remember, your escape from the BAD SUGAR trap is for you and you alone. The selfish pursuit of a way of eating and living that is best for you is a wonderful thing. But being free from BAD SUGAR *leaves so much amazing, nutritious, healthy food in your life – your family won't even notice if you help them by influencing their eating for the better.*

EATING AND LIVING HEALTHILY

Breakfast can comprise beautiful fresh fruit – the true breakfast of champions. The conditions are perfect: your stomach will be empty after a night's sleep and, having gained all those nutrients from that delicious, juicy, energy-giving fruit, you will not need to eat again until lunchtime.

Next time you're food shopping, forget the cereals – nearly all breakfast cereals have a high GL – and head instead to the fruit section. Notice the aroma; what other section of a supermarket actually smells enticing? And by the way, you'll find the aroma even more appealing at a market stall or a greengrocer's, where the fruit tends to be riper. Your eyes will behold a vast array of beautiful-looking fruit, more attractive than any other food display you'll find, and you can take your pick from all manner of different fruits, each with their own aroma, texture and flavour.

No other breakfast can offer the variety fruit does. Eat it raw to maintain the nutritional value and you'll be amazed that you don't need to eat piles of it to satisfy your hunger.

If you really don't fancy fruit for breakfast then you have other choices. Eggs may be a secondary food but there's no reason why you shouldn't enjoy them with some chopped salad in the morning – cooked however you like them depending on how you feel.

When it comes to lunch and dinner, don't settle for boring salads. Make sure you have as much, or as little, variety as you like. Take pleasure in mixing different salads, vegetables and fruits. Don't forget, secondary foods, such as ham, chicken and fish can add variety and taste also. Just make sure they are not the main feature. Aim to have small portions of those and make up for it with wonderful full salads and vegetables.

A small handful of nuts or seeds is a lovely end to a meal.

Try this for a while and you will quickly find that it becomes second nature – or rather first nature, since this is the way we were designed to eat.

Having the occasional fry-up or steak meal won't cause you a problem, but do try to always have a wonderful, tasty fresh salad with as many meals as you can.

You will feel the extra energy from your new way of eating, you'll see the benefits in the mirror and, without the lows of addiction to BAD SUGAR, you will feel happier all round.

You may well feel inclined to take up some form of regular exercise. If you do, make sure it's for pleasure and not to lose weight; otherwise it will become a hardship, like a diet, and it will be self-defeating. Exercising for pleasure is a wonderful thing for both mind and body and you're bound to become more active now that you are no longer bogged down with BAD SUGAR. As a result you will have a bigger appetite. This is nothing to worry about as long as you fuel up with the right kind of foods, which deliver their calories in a usable form and don't get stored as fat.

Moving your body is a wonderful thing. Swapping the drive through traffic for the freedom of a commute that allows you to walk as well as take the train or bus will make you feel like a million dollars and do amazing things for your stress levels. If you love the gym, great – but why take and hour and a half out of your day to sweat in the gym when you could spend the same time walking to and from work?

The cycle of healthy eating and activity is not something you have to work at. You will feel it working for you right from the start. Your natural fuel gauge will control the balance between intake and output and as long as you keep putting the right fuel in, the natural cycle will keep you fit and healthy without any special effort required.

EAT YOUR FAVOURITE FOODS

Without any sense of sacrifice you may well find that you cut out all sorts of other secondary foods that you used to think were your favourites, but, as you know, that is not the basis of the method.

Non-vegetarians tend to assume that being vegetarian means making a sacrifice. You haven't had to make any sacrifices. If there are some secondary foods, like meat and dairy, that you don't want to live without, you can go ahead and eat them, as long as you remember that primary foods – fresh fruit, vegetables, nuts and seeds – should form the cornerstone of your diet for life.

If you do that you will spend the rest of your life enjoying what you eat and feeling good about yourself because

YOU'RE IN CONTROL AND YOU'RE FREE!

------------ SUMMARY ------------

- Enjoy the death throes of the Little Monster.
- Prepare yourself for down days – you'll cope better free from *BAD SUGAR.*
- Discover the joys of a fruit-only breakfast.
- What you eat is now up to you – you're in control.

Chapter 20

USEFUL REMINDERS

The references in this chapter are for people who have read the book, freed themselves from BAD SUGAR addiction and just need to remind themselves of a certain point. If you've jumped straight to this page without reading the rest of the book, the method will not work. Please go back to the start of Chapter 1 and read the whole book from start to finish.

THE INSTRUCTIONS

Easyway is a proven method for curing addiction. It requires no willpower and there is no painful withdrawal period. All you have to do is follow all the instructions.

1. FOLLOW ALL THE INSTRUCTIONS. (CH1)

2. KEEP AN OPEN MIND. (CH2)

3. BEGIN WITH A FEELING OF ELATION. (CH3)

4. IGNORE ANY ADVICE THAT GOES AGAINST NATURE'S GUIDE. (CH6)

5. FREE YOURSELF FROM SLAVERY TO YOUR PRESENT EATING HABITS. (CH7)

6. DISREGARD ANY PRECONCEIVED TARGET WEIGHT. (CH8)

7. AVOID EATING UNLESS YOU'RE HUNGRY. (CH8)

8. NEVER DOUBT YOUR DECISION TO QUIT. (CH9)

9. IGNORE THE ADVICE OF ANYONE WHO CLAIMS TO HAVE QUIT BY WILLPOWER. (CH10)

10. IGNORE ALL ADVICE AND INFLUENCES THAT CONFLICT WITH Easyway. (CH11)

11. GO FOR IT! (CH15)

12. GL IS ONLY A GUIDE – TO BE SURE THAT YOU ARE FREE FROM BAD SUGAR ADDICTION CUT OUT REFINED SUGAR ITEMS, PROCESSED CARB ITEMS, AND STARCHY CARB ITEMS (THIS INCLUDES PRETTY MUCH ALL READY-MADE MEALS AND PROCESSED FOODS). (CH16)

ENJOY LIFE FREE FROM BAD SUGAR!

ALLEN CARR'S EASYWAY CLINICS

The following list indicates the countries where Allen Carr's Easyway To Stop Smoking Clinics are operational at the time of printing.

Check www.allencarr.com for latest additions to this list.

The success rate at the clinics, based on the three-month money-back guarantee, is over 90 percent.

Selected clinics also offer sessions that deal with alcohol, other drugs, and weight issues. Please check with your nearest clinic, listed on the following pages, for details.

Allen Carr's Easyway guarantees that you will find it easy to stop at the clinics or your money back.

JOIN US!

Allen Carr's Easyway Clinics have spread throughout the world with incredible speed and success. Our global network now covers more than 150 cities in over 50 countries. This amazing growth has been achieved entirely organically. Former addicts, just like you, were so impressed by the ease with which they stopped that they felt inspired to contact us to see how they could bring the method to their region.

If you feel the same, contact us for details on how to become an Allen Carr's Easyway To Stop Smoking or an Allen Carr's Easyway To Stop Drinking franchisee.

Email us at: join-us@allencarr.com including your full name, postal address, and region of interest.

SUPPORT US!

No, don't send us money!

You have achieved something really marvelous. Every time we hear of someone escaping from the sinking ship, we get a feeling of enormous sattisfaction.

It would give us great pleasure to hear that you have freed yourself from the slavery of addiction, so please visit the following web page where you can tell us of your success, inspire others to follow in your footsteps and hear about ways you can help to spread the word.

www.allencarr.com/444/support-us

You can "like" our Facebook page here
www.facebook.com/AllenCarr

Together, we can help further Allen Carr's mission: to cure the world of addiction.

LONDON CLINIC AND WORLDWIDE HEAD OFFICE

Park House, 14 Pepys Road,

Raynes Park, London SW20 8NH

Tel: +44 (0)20 8944 7761

Fax: +44 (0)20 8944 8619

Email: mail@allencarr.com

Website: **www.allencarr.com**

Therapists: John Dicey, Colleen Dwyer, Crispin Hay, Emma
  Hudson, Rob Fielding, Sam Carroll, Sam Bonner

Worldwide Press Office

Contact: John Dicey

Tel: +44 (0)7970 88 44 52

Email: media@allencarr.com

UK Clinic Network

We have clinics throughout the UK. Call 0800 389 2115 or visit
www.allencarr.com

Worldwide Clinic Network

We also have clinics in the following countries, but the list is
constantly growing. For details of existing clinics and out latest
additions, visit www.allencarr.com

AUSTRALIA	MAURITIUS
AUSTRIA	MEXICO
BELGIUM	NETHERLANDS
BULGARIA	NEW ZEALAND
CHILE	NORWAY
COLOMBIA	PERU
CZECH REPUBLIC	POLAND
DENMARK	PORTUGAL
FINLAND	ROMANIA
FRANCE	RUSSIA
GERMANY	SERBIA
GREECE	SINGAPORE
GUATEMALA	SLOVAKIA
HONG KONG	SLOVENIA
HUNGARY	SOUTH AFRICA
ICELAND	SOUTH KOREA
INDIA	SPAIN
IRELAND	SWEDEN
ISRAEL	SWITZERLAND
ITALY	TURKEY
JAPAN	UKRAINE
LEBANON	USA
LITHUANIA	

The number of countries we cover keeps increasing all the time, so please check www.allencarr.com for our latest list.

OTHER ALLEN CARR PUBLICATIONS

Allen Carr's revolutionary Easyway method is available in a wide variety of formats, including digitally as audiobooks and ebooks, and has been successfully applied to a broad range of subjects. For more information about Easyway publications, please visit shop.allencarr.com

ALLEN CARR BOOKS

Lose Weight Now
(with hypnotherapy CD)
ISBN: 978-1-84837-720-2

No More Diets
ISBN: 978-1-84837-554-3

The Easyweigh to Lose Weight
ISBN: 978-0-71819-472-7

The Easy Way for Women to Lose
Weight
ISBN: 978-1-78599-303-9

Stop Smoking Now
(with hypnotherapy CD)
ISBN: 978-1-84837-373-0

Stop Smoking with Allen Carr
(with 70-minute audio CD)
ISBN: 978-1-84858-997-1

Your Personal Stop Smoking Plan
ISBN: 978-1-78404-501-2

Easyway Express: Stop Smoking and
Quit E-cigarettes
Ebook

The Illustrated Easy Way to Stop
Smoking
ISBN: 978-1-84837-930-5

Finally Free!
ISBN: 978-1-84858-979-7

The Easy Way for Women to Stop
Smoking
ISBN: 978-1-84837-464-5

The Illustrated Easy Way for Women to
Stop Smoking
ISBN: 978-1-78212-495-5

How to Be a Happy Non-smoker
Ebook

Smoking Sucks
(Parent Guide with 16-page comic)
Ebook

No More Ashtrays
ISBN: 978-1-84858-083-1

The Little Book of Quitting
ISBN: 978-0-14028-900-8

The Only Way to Stop Smoking
Permanently
ISBN: 978-1-40591-638-7

The Easy Way to Stop Smoking
ISBN: 978-1-40592-331-6

How to Stop Your Child Smoking
ISBN: 978-0-14027-836-1

Stop Drinking Now
(with hypnotherapy CD)
ISBN: 978-1-84837-982-4

The Illustrated Easy Way to Stop
Drinking
ISBN: 978-1-78404-504-3

The Easy Way to Control Alcohol
ISBN: 978-1-84837-465-2

The Easy Way for Women to Stop
Drinking
ISBN: 978-1-78599-193-6

No More Hangovers
ISBN: 978-1-84837-555-0

The Easy Way to Stop Gambling
ISBN: 978-1-78212-448-1

No More Gambling
Ebook

No More Worrying
ISBN: 978-1-84837-826-1

Get Out of Debt Now
ISBN: 978-1-84837-981-7

No More Debt
Ebook

No More Fear of Flying
ISBN: 978-1-78404-279-0

The Easy Way to Enjoy Flying
ISBN: 978-0-71819-438-3

Burning Ambition
ISBN: 978-0-14103-030-2

The Nicotine Conspiracy
Ebook

Packing It In The Easy Way
(the autobiography)
ISBN: 978-0-14101-517-0

Want Easyway on your smartphone or tablet?

Search for "Allen Carr" in your app store.

Easyway publications are also available as audiobooks.

Visit shop.allencarr.com to find out more.